CONTENTS

INTRODUCTION

If terrorism is even more of a problem in two hundred years' time than it is now, archaeologists in Texas will be in trouble. While I was working with a church in Lubbock, Texas, I spent some time in the church's library. Around the top of the room were air vents which blew hot air into the room and I was fascinated by a sign that hung above one of them. It said, 'Please do not adjust these vents, they are set to blow up'!

Knowing that America and Britain do not use the English language in the same way, and being aware of what sort of building I was in, I think I worked out what that notice meant! But if the church falls into disrepair and, two hundred years from now, somebody excavating it comes into the library and sees the sign, he may think he's discovered the headquarters of a guerrilla organisation and that the vents are booby-trapped!

Reading the New Testament presents the same

sort of difficulties. We are trying to make sense of letters and other documents that were written not just two hundred but two thousand years ago – in another culture and another language.

So, why bother?

Paul's letter to Timothy, the young pastor of a growing church, is vital reading for anyone who wants to learn more about using his or her gifts to serve God. His message is for every Christian as he or she goes about daily life.

As we draw out the main themes within the letter we will discover that the questions Timothy had about the Christian life and how to use his gifts effectively were no different from those we face today.

Build on the principles Paul gives here, and you will be well on the way to a life of fruitful service.

word for **TODAY**

GROWING *your* gifts

2 Timothy: Ministry in today's world

STEPHEN GAUKROGER

SCRIPTURE UNION
130 CITY ROAD, LONDON EC1V 2NJ

© Stephen Gaukroger 1991

First published in 1991 by Scripture Union,
130 City Road, London EC1V 2NJ.

British Library Cataloguing in Publication Data
Gaukroger, Stephen 1954 –
Growing your gifts
1. Bible. N. T. 2 Timothy. Critical studies
I. Title II. series
227. 8406
ISBN 0 86201 630 4

Scripture quotations in this publication are from the Holy Bible, New International
Version. Copyright © 1973, 1978, 1984 International Bible Society. Published by
Hodder & Stoughton.

Phototypeset by Input Typesetting Ltd, London SW19 8DR
Printed and bound in Great Britain by Cox & Wyman Ltd, Reading.

Thanks to . . .

Becky, my editor, for her hours of hard work and
constant support; numerous friends around the
country who encouraged me in my writing;
Stopsley Baptist Church for being such willing
guinea-pigs for so much of this material;
JLM, BJ, CE and SR, whom I love.

Dedicated to . . .

CBS, RTK and DWP – valued members of my
fellowship group.

1
DISCOVERING
YOUR
GIFTS

It's the end of a busy day. There is a knock at my study door and my last 'visitor' has come, a young woman interested in finding out more about leadership. After talking for a while I discover that's not why she's come at all. Years ago her father sexually abused her and the emotional and spiritual scars have not healed.

Three lads in their late teens phone up in the middle of the night, obviously the worse for drink: 'We thought you could tell us about God.'

A letter arrives on my desk: 'The Lord has shown me that he's not going to bless your ministry. And he's told me why . . .'

A man who thinks he might have AIDS phones up. 'Can I come to church? . . . Is it all right if I bring my boyfriend?'

As I think about the problems that crop up in my role as pastor, preacher and teacher, I'm relieved to know that I didn't take on the task simply because I felt like it! Rather, I'm doing it because God gave me the basic gifts and called me to use and develop them in this way.

GIFTED?

From time to time people come to me and say, 'What can I do in the church? I don't know if I've got any real gifts but I feel I'd like to help somehow.' Many people doubt whether they really do have any gifts that can be of use to God, but the New Testament tells us that God has given each of us gifts to use and develop in his service: 'Each one should use whatever gift he has received to serve others, faithfully administering God's grace in its various forms' (1 Peter 4:10). These gifts may develop in us as our spiritual life develops, or they may be given to us as a result of prayer or the laying on of hands.

The New Testament spells out an amazing variety of gifts. You will find them in, for example, Romans 12:6–8; 1 Corinthians 12:4–11, 27–31; and Ephesians 4:11–13. The sort of gifts mentioned divide into three main types.

• There are gifts of 'caring': encouraging others; showing kindness; giving pastoral care; serving others.

• There are gifts of 'thinking and talking': prophecy; bringing messages of wisdom; bringing messages of knowledge; the ability to distinguish between those messages that come from God and those that do not;

speaking in tongues – spiritual languages; the ability to explain what is being said in those languages; teaching; evangelism.

● There are also gifts of 'doing': leadership; faith; the power to heal; the power to work miracles; administration; helping others practically; sharing resources with others in need.

Perhaps you are gifted in caring for others – you are good at encouraging others or at making people new to the church feel at home. Perhaps you have gifts of thinking and talking: you can get your mind round ideas and help other people understand them; you are able to give good advice when asked for it. Perhaps you have gifts of 'doing': if someone needs something mended, organised or fixed, they come to you knowing that you will make it happen!

If you are not sure what gifts you have, take a look at the gift identification questionnaire at the back of this book. This will help you to pinpoint the sort of areas where God might want to use you in the life of the church and the community.

GROWING

Sometimes we look at how other Christians are able to serve the church and their community, and we think, 'I could never do that! I've not got much in the way of gifts.' It is true that God has given each of us particular gifts but at the moment they might just be gift 'seeds', waiting for us to water and feed them so that they can grow into something powerful and useful.

These seeds will begin to grow as we dedicate all that we are to God and as we step out in faith to use the little bits of gift we know we have. As we grow more like Christ in our character, so he can use those gifts more fully. And as we use them more fully, so the seedling gifts grow into strong, mature, effective gifts to use in his service.

Finding your niche

Once we have discovered our main area of gifting, we will want to know how God wants us to use those gifts. It is important to know that we are using them in the way that will be most effective.

Paul's opening line in his letter to Timothy shows that he was sure he was using his gifts for speaking and teaching in the way God wanted him to:

> 'Paul, an apostle of Christ Jesus by the will of God, according to the promise of life that is in Christ Jesus.'

Paul was convinced that he was to use those gifts to tell others about Jesus. He calls himself an apostle, literally a 'sent one', and says that it was 'the will of God' that he should take on this task.

How could Paul be so sure? We tend to spend hours agonising about what is 'the right' thing to do when we are faced with a change of job, a house move or which school to send the children to. How can we tell what is the right course of action for putting our gifts to good use?

One way is to think what particular 'ministry' you could take on because of the gifts you have. The gifts are what we have; the ministry is the way we use them and this can be either within or outside the fellowship. Although every Christian has gifts to use for the good of the church fellowship, most of us spend most of our time in a secular job or at home and in our local community, and our gifts can be of use there too. In fact, it may be that our ministry will mostly be to colleagues and our families. If, as a teacher, business-man, assembly-line worker, accountant or homemaker you are using the gifts God has given you in a way that shows people something of him, you are God's 'minister' in that place.

If you have teaching gifts, it may be that you should be developing a teaching ministry in the church – but perhaps your school teaching job should be your main ministry.

You may not be called to use your gifts of caring in full-time pastoral ministry but those gifts could be well used in visiting the elderly or in opening up the church on weekdays as a drop-in centre for those who are lonely, or by offering support and encouragement to colleagues at work.

Do you play a musical instrument? Perhaps you could develop that gift in helping to lead worship in the church or in a housegroup. Or it may be that you could give something more valuable as a Christian if you invested your time and talents with a local non-Christian music group.

Do you get heated and angry about social issues – the state of our prisons, the effects of the poll tax, the number of abortions carried out each year? It may be that God is calling you to use your gifts to minister outside the fellowship, prison visiting, campaigning, or forming support groups for expectant mums. Or perhaps your ministry will be as union representative in your office or factory.

As we think about the gifts we have, it is good to talk over with our church leaders and with friends who know us well, exactly how we can begin to develop them or use them more fully. Usually, the right decision here will be confirmed to us by a deep sense of peace and security.

This doesn't mean we always *feel peaceful* when we are serving God in the place to which he has called us – often quite the reverse! We will probably experience pressure, problems and even persecution from Satan. Let's face it, *he* certainly doesn't want us to be using our gifts effectively and, when we are, he'll do his level best to stop us enjoying it!

You may need to try a number of areas before

you feel you have found your main sphere of ministry. You may, of course, have gifts in several different areas. In this case, church leaders and friends may be able to point to the tasks most in need of being done, whether in the community, at work or in the fellowship, and help you to plan where and how to put those gifts to use.

RIGHT REASONS

Before his conversion, Paul had been a 'religious studies' teacher in Jerusalem. He had been educated by Gamaliel, a highly respected Rabbi, and had gone to the best universities of his day. He had even been born into a city famous for its great intellectuals, Tarsus. But he didn't for one moment think that his academic qualifications gave him the right to teach others about Christ. Two other things did that.

Knowing Jesus

The first was his personal meeting with Christ on the road to Damascus. Paul was temporarily blinded in that dramatic event but when he was able to see again it was not just physically. For the very first time, despite all his years of studying the Old Testament law, he could see spiritually.

We can know all there is to know *about* Jesus but if we don't know him personally we will not be able to introduce others to him. In Christian service it's *who* you know, not *what* you know, that matters most. I can think of dozens of people who have proved this.

There's the young wife who was full of enthusiasm for the Lord after her conversion. She had no theological training at all but she knew Jesus and nothing would stop her telling others about him. She had a gift for spotting and doing practical things to help her friends and neighbours. While she helped out or made them coffee she would talk about Jesus.

There's the insurance salesman who gets to the end of his patter then adds, 'Actually, I'm a Christian and I think the greatest form of insurance you can have is to know Jesus', and gives his client a book explaining the Christian faith.

There's the elderly person whose special ministry is prayer. She spends so much time with Jesus that he seems to radiate from her. Being with her is a real encouragement and inspiration.

Being called

Secondly, even though Paul had all the right skills, they were not enough to make him an apostle. His ministry was something to which he had to be called. Being smart at sums, clever with kids or a genius with groups doesn't automatically mean you should volunteer to be church accountant, help in the Sunday School or lead a house group! It is likely that God will use those natural gifts that you have – but the call must come from him.

GOD'S HELP GUARANTEED

God guarantees to give us his help in using, day by day, the gifts he has given us. This present of help comes wrapped up in three parcels labelled 'grace', 'mercy' and 'peace'. As Paul began to write to Timothy he wanted to remind him of all that God had ready to give him. He also wanted to be sure Timothy knew that it is only because God has already given us grace, mercy and peace that ministry of any kind is possible:

> 'To Timothy, my dear son:
> Grace, mercy and peace from God the Father
> and Christ Jesus our Lord.'

In other words, 'remember how it all started,' says Paul. 'God took you from being outside his kingdom and gave you new life in Christ: that's grace! What's more, Jesus didn't *have* to die for you but, because he loves you so much, he would have done so even if you were the only sinner in the world: that's mercy! And he wants you to be sure of these things and of his constant care: that's peace!' As we prepare for ministry in the fellowship, home or our work places, we can depend on these three things to act both as first aid kit and as tool kit.

A hymn that was often sung in the church in which I grew up began, 'There is a balm in Gilead.' As a teenager, I couldn't for the life of me figure out what it meant! It was, in fact, a quote from Jeremiah 8:22; the 'balm' was a kind of ointment or eye salve that came from Gilead, an area of Israel famous for its spices and medicinal herbs. It was just the thing for soothing eyes that were irritated by the dust and grit of a hot, dry country. What Jeremiah was getting at was that the promises of God to his struggling and suffering people were the spiritual equivalent of that soothing, healing balm of Gilead. They were to remember those promises and be encouraged and renewed by them.

When we feel unsure of ourselves, uncertain that God really has called us to serve him, afraid of what it might involve, we need to 'apply' these gifts of grace, mercy and peace to ourselves. We need to absorb them until we can *feel* God's love for us and are assured of his power for the task.

There may be times in your ministry when you are depressed by criticism, overwhelmed by work and floored by the complexity of the people for whom you are caring. There are times when life at home is chaotic and demanding. Whatever problems and tensions you face, God wants to give you his grace to cope with them, the certainty of his constant love in the midst of them, and the peace that comes from trusting him to resolve them in his own time and way.

GETTING STARTED

It can take a lot of courage to launch out into using our gifts in a particular form of ministry, whether it is accepting speaking engagements, taking the initiative to visit elderly folk who cannot get out very much, offering Christian counsel to people when they tell you about their problems, or getting involved with running the local mother and toddler group. We need the help of others! Ask a few friends to support you in the following ways:

• Before you take the plunge: in helping you to think about what it will involve – in time, in skills, for your family – and to help you prepare.

• During your first attempts: to pray for you and to cheer you on.

• After your first attempts: to encourage you, help you to assess which things went well and which were not quite so good, and to help come up with ways to do even better next time.

2

SECRETS OF SUCCESSFUL SERVICE

It seems that all the churches Timothy established turned out to be strong and permanent. Paul's letter to him gives us four clues as to why Timothy was able to use his gift for preaching so successfully:

> 'I thank God, whom I serve, as my forefathers did, with a clear conscience, as night and day I constantly remember you in my prayers. Recalling your tears, I long to see you, so that I may be filled with joy. I have been reminded of your sincere faith, which first lived in your grandmother Lois and in your mother Eunice and, I am persuaded, now lives in you also. For this reason I remind you to fan into flame the gift of God, which is in you through the laying on of my hands. For God did not give us a spirit of timidity, but a spirit of power, of love and of self-discipline.' *2 Timothy 1:3–7*

1 PRAYER

Firstly, Timothy was surrounded by prayer. Paul wanted him to know how deeply committed he was to his well-being and that he was always praying for him. Paul could encourage him to get on and do his bit for the kingdom only because he was backing Timothy up with his own hard work of prayer.

Timothy's ministry was undergirded by the prayers of many others too, without doubt including those of Mum and Grandma! The secret of an effective ministry is the prayer of the people of God. In the long run, our ministry will only be as powerful as the prayers of those who pray for us. In the same way, a preacher or teacher can influence others by his or her skills of communication but the ability to build up a church is given by God. Even the most gifted speaker simply doesn't have the skill to do this without God's help.

When I was in the States I watched, with interest and amazement, some American television. For a start, the home in which I was staying had a television with eighty-three channels! I heard a variety of people preach and teach, some of them riveting, brilliant communicators who hold massive audiences in the palm of their hand. I also heard of a number of other superb communicators; crowds had flocked to hear them off screen and they had seemed all set for a successful television ministry. But today they are nowhere to be seen, largely because they depended only on the skills of oratory and good communication. Their audiences were interested simply in the fireworks of a dramatic performance. The prayers of God's people were not undergirding those ministries, helping to transform them into something that would have eternal effectiveness.

If you have already found your ministry 'niche' in the church fellowship or are still thinking about it, ask a couple of friends to be your prayer partners, praying with you and for you. Keep them up to date with what you are planning or doing and what you want to see happen as a result. Then pray it into reality!

The same goes for your work and witness at home or in your secular job. If you feel you have reached a dead end in terms of being effective for God there, perhaps the answer is to enlist the support of others to pray with you about it. It is also very helpful to have a prayer partner who will pray with you about persistent problems at work or home. When you have to decide how to react to fraud or sexual harrassment at work, or are expected to cover up for the mistakes of colleagues by lying and deceit, how do you cope? Who helps you think it through? A prayer partner whom you can trust with these problems is invaluable.

In addition, why not determine now to pray regularly for those who are using their gifts in some of the 'front-line' ways – in evangelism, youth work or teaching, for instance? Really pray! Your prayers could be the key to their success. There is no such thing as 'one man ministry'; without the active, prayerful support of all God's people, there can be no ministry at all. When we finally meet God, will he have to explain that our churches have been so weak because the people of God never really prayed? We need to commit ourselves to praying that each other's ministries of 'caring', 'talking and thinking' and 'doing' will be powerful and effective in our communities.

2 ROLE MODELS

Timothy's ministry was successful because he had good role models. He grew up in a home where Jesus was known as Lord and, later, he was able to work with Paul, watching and learning from him.

Role models in the home

Many Christian families suffer because Mum or Dad is so 'committed' to the work of the church or so 'conscientious' about his or her day-to-day work that the children don't see much of them. Timothy, by contrast, seems to have grown up with adults in whom he could see the power of the living God at work. 'Lois', the name of Timothy's grandmother, means 'desirable' and 'Eunice', the name of his mother, means 'good victory'. He saw the gospel lived out at home in a way that was both attractive and powerful.

Children naturally copy the behaviour and attitudes of adults. I am at the stage of fatherhood now where my wife often has to tell me off. Apparently, I am teaching our small daughters to do things their mother doesn't think they should! I don't teach them deliberately – most of the time – but there are little things I say, gestures I make and things I do that call forth the comment, 'Now we don't want Bethany and Cara doing *that*, do we?!' I can't very well say to my children, 'Don't do that!' if, two minutes later, *I'm* going to do it!

As we observe children and see their family life, we can often predict how they are going to grow up. Already at seven, eight or nine, they are mirroring the bad habits and attitudes of their parents. Their attitudes to Christian things are becoming sour and twisted because they are growing up in a home where, although the family members go to church, the risen Christ is not known in a loving, gentle and attractive way.

Today we can get almost anything instantly, from coffee to credit. But we can't conjure up instant Christian character in our children. It is tempting to leave that to the church fellowship. We take our children along as though we were putting scrambled egg in the microwave. Two minutes teaching in Sunday School then 'ping!' out they come as strong, spiritually mature Christians ready to give a lead to the next generation. Or so we hope!

Lois and Eunice put time and patience into nourishing Timothy's young life. We cannot over-estimate the impact on a person's future ministry of a godly Christian home.

Role models in the church

Paul comes across as amazingly arrogant at times! 'Timothy,' he says, 'you know all about me. You have seen my life, my purpose for living, my faith. You have seen how patient I am! How loving I am! How enduring I am! You have even seen me suffer persecution . . . Now model your life on mine':

> 'You, however, know all about my teaching,
> my way of life, my purpose, faith, patience,
> love, endurance, persecutions, sufferings – what
> kinds of things happened to me in Antioch,
> Iconium and Lystra, the persecutions I
> endured . . . But as for you, continue in what
> you have learned and have become convinced
> of, because you know those from whom you
> learned it.'
>
> *2 Timothy 3:10–14*

Paul was not claiming to be perfect but he was right to encourage Timothy to follow his example. We know we should follow the example of Jesus but sometimes we need a model and guide who is easier to 'see'. Who can we look to for this sort of role model?

● The historical 'greats': people like Martin Luther, John Wesley, George Muller or Lord Shaftesbury. Get hold of their biographies and find out what it was that made them great.

● The contemporary 'greats': people like Billy Graham, Mother Teresa, Eva Burrows, Desmond Tutu – people whose ministries have made them nationally and internationally famous. What motivates them? How do they cope with difficulties? What are the secrets of their success?

● The mature Christians you will find in your own church fellowship: people who are emotionally secure and spiritually wise. Some will be particularly good listeners; what makes them so? Some always seem to have the right thing to say to someone who needs guidance; why's that? Some have the knack of making you feel welcome and at home; how do they do it? We can learn much simply by observing how others have put their gifts to use.

As well as looking for role models on which to pattern our own ministries, we need to be aware that in the church family and in the wider community too, people are looking to us to demonstrate the truth of what we say. My wife once told me, 'You're a model husband.' I felt rather pleased about that! As I basked in the warm glow it gave me I looked up 'model' in the dictionary. This is what it said: 'Model: small imitation of the real thing'! That can be the problem with us; we often do not show what real Christianity is all about. Unless our lives model what we say, our words will carry no weight.

Perhaps your children have grown up or maybe you do not have children, even so we all have some contact with young people, especially those in our church fellowships. Although we may not be their parents, they see us as 'The Church'. They draw conclusions about Christianity from what they see in us. If they want to know whether a particular kind of behaviour is acceptable, they look at us to find out.

If we are going to help our young people towards effective future ministries, we must set them the kind of example that Paul set Timothy.

3   CONTINUING RENEWAL

At some time, Paul had laid hands on Timothy, recognising his gifts and sending him out to use them for God's glory. Now that Timothy was hitting problems Paul was concerned that his enthusiasm might begin to tail off, just as a roaring fire slowly dies down when the flames bite into wet wood. So he reminds Timothy of that very special event when he was commissioned for his task and specially equipped to do it. He probably guessed that the memory of it would rekindle Timothy's determination and commitment:

> '. . . fan into flame the gift of God, which is in
> you through the laying on of my hands. For
> God did not give us a spirit of timidity, but a
> spirit of power, of love and of self-disipline.'
> *2 Timothy 1: 6–7*

Camp fires have a habit of going out while you are not watching them – especially if they took hours of hard labour to light! There's nothing else for it but to get down on all fours and puff some life into them until the dying embers flicker into flame again. In the same way, in Christian ministry it's easy to get so bogged down by the wet wood of routine, tedious tasks, the everyday and the hum-drum that we run out of spiritual power to cope with them.

We know what this means in practice. Doing the washing up suddenly seems so much more exciting than planning tomorrow night's house group meeting! Or you suggest that it would be a good idea to hold the deacons' meeting at your house so that you could carry on painting the skirting boards while you talk. Or you 'forget' to visit old Mr Smith because there's that film on TV you really want to see. Our creativity easily dries up and we realise we are doing those tasks, for which we are gifted, out of habit rather than heartfelt commitment.

Sometimes it is simply the busyness of our daily lives – the pressure of circumstances, trouble, tensions or stress of a variety of kinds – that leads us into a mediocre spiritual life. That flame of spiritual vitality we once had has died down. That touch from the Holy Spirit when someone laid hands on us seems far away. The conversion experience in which we felt so close to God or the time when God moved into our life in a new way, now hardly seems real.

If we are simply going through the motions of

spiritual life, we need to make the time to fan it back into reality. There must be a freshness and vitality about our own walk with the Lord if our ministry to others is to be effective.

The good news is that flagging ministries can be fanned back into flame. The bad news is that it takes a major act of will, strengthened and encouraged by the Holy Spirit. If you know this is what you need to do, share it with one or two trusted friends and pray with them. It may be that you are simply too busy and drained of *all* energy and enthusiasm, not just enthusiasm for using your gifts for the Lord. Your friends may be able to help you reorder your priorities or see that you take a break. Perhaps you need to be reassured that you *are* gifted in the ways you think you are, and are using those gifts in the place God wants you to. Sometimes other people can see that more clearly than we can ourselves. Ask your friends to be honest with you; encourage them not to let you off the hook until your ministry is revived – and don't give up!

4 THE HOLY SPIRIT

Very often when I suggest to particular people that they consider training for housegroup leadership, they respond with something like, 'Oh, I couldn't do that; I haven't got my own act together yet!' Or, 'I'm not spiritual enough.' Those may be very true self-observations, but they should not stop a person from taking on that leadership role! I encourage them instead to trust the judgment of those who have spotted the gift in them, and to trust God to work through them, despite any inadequacies they feel. The attitude, 'I'm not good enough,' is actually an important one to maintain; it is only when we realise our own limitations that we are prepared to let God take the reins and work through us.

Timothy was young and probably not at all sure of his own abilities. When he took a cold, hard look at the responsibilities of his ministry he got frightened. But God had promised to give him power, love and self-discipline – vital gifts if his ministry was to be effective. The Lord wants to give those same three things to us, too, for the areas of service to which he has called us. The Spirit within us is *powerful*; when he is directing operations the work will be done quickly and expertly. His Spirit will give us *love*, so that the power is under control; and *self-discipline*, so that our weaknesses are kept in check and do not undermine our ministry.

Power

Before a new building can be put up, the old building on the site must be smashed to the ground and the rubbish cleared. In the same way, the Spirit of Christ has to do some demolition work in us before he can build something solid in us and with us. God hates all the sin in our lives and he wants to destroy it. Like the prophet Jeremiah, we are called 'to uproot and tear down, to destroy and overthrow' and only then 'to build and to plant' (Jeremiah 1:10). Selfishness, pride, fear, even feelings of insecurity need to be swept away if God is to help us grow in the use of our gifts.

The same can be true of a church fellowship as a whole. To begin with, most of our churches need a demolition contractor in to deal with their outdated organisations. It is easy to cling on to 'what we have always done' simply because we feel secure with the predictable. But might some of our many meetings actually be hindering God's work rather than achieving it? At Stopsley we decided to close down a midweek Ladies' meeting because it no longer seemed to be meeting a need. We also wound up, with sadness, the Girls' Brigade. After a time each was replaced with more appropriate alternatives.

There may be destructive attitudes in a church which need to be rooted out before the ministry of the fellowship as a whole can be effective. In large churches where it is easy to form hasty opinions of others, gossip, back-biting and sniping may need to be smashed down and broken. Smaller churches, on the other hand, often suffer from a false sense of ownership on the part of their elders or deacons: 'It's *my* church!' is sometimes their real feeling.

If we allow the demolition contractor in, we are forced to let go of our own secure holds and reach out instead towards the marvellous future God has in mind for us, whatever that may be. As we clear the site of all its clutter we will be able to gauge more clearly the ministry goals that *Christ* has for us and for *his* church.

Love

When the demolition work is complete the ground needs to be levelled out so that new work can begin. Demolition is costly and painful but God works to change us gently and lovingly, at a pace we can handle. Demolition work will need to be done in us throughout our lives but, as God does it, he smooths out all the brokenness and pain we feel and gives us the security from which to launch out into new areas of service. He also develops this same love in us so that we can use it in our ministries to bring healing and encouragement to others.

Self-discipline

Thirdly, we need self-discipline if we are to mature as Christians and use our gifts to build up the body of Christ.

Western culture today looks on self-discipline as something deviant. We are bombarded by a hundred voices urging us to take up the latest fads and fashions. 'The good life is yours for the asking! Just buy this aftershave, that car, this box of chocolates and the world will be at your feet!' It all looks and sounds so easy! But building a mature Christian faith that will stand up under pressure takes hard work and self-discipline.

Some of us can get stuck into a project which will take a month or two, but commitment to Christian living demands our attention week after week, year after year, until we die! Most of us find that our enthusiasm tails off very easily. Many of us, for instance, are bad at making time to read the Bible and to pray regularly – though we are very good at talking about it! We need the self-discipline of a devotional life which is feeding on God's word; a tongue under control – free from gossip, lies and negative cynicism; an emotional life under God's authority and of a commitment to other people which goes beyond our feelings. Self-discipline enables us to do something because it is *right*, not because we necessarily feel like doing it.

A building worth having is not built over night, nor haphazardly and in a hurry – the bricks thrown together crookedly, the roof at five different angles, the windows all askew! It demands careful, painstaking work or we will soon see the cracks appear. God's work in us will take the whole of our life but will last for all eternity. In the same way, those who are called to build in the lives of others, in Christ's name, need to be determined and patient builders. If things have not 'happened' in one or two years, or even in six months or six weeks, we can begin to wonder if there was any point in it. Then it is a short step to giving up and going back to what is safe and predictable.

If we want to see God's glory descend into our churches so that the miraculous happens and individuals become filled with the Spirit of Christ, we must keep on looking to God to do his work in us and through us.

3

A LIFE INVESTMENT

After much prayer and enthusiastic cajolling, Carole has at last persuaded her friend, Sandra, to go with her to an evangelistic service at church. There is an 'appeal' at the end and, to Carole's delight, Sandra decides to become a Christian. Carole goes off rejoicing, glad to have been able to add another sheep to the fold.

But Sandra, now left to fend for herself as a new Christian, stands as much chance of survival as an ice cube in the Sahara! As struggles with sceptical friends, old habits and pressures of time hot up, that initial sense of commitment begins to melt away. Why isn't it lasting? What's going wrong?

In his book, *Discipleship*[1], David Watson puts his finger on the problem: 'Christians in the West have largely neglected what it means to be a *disciple of Christ*.' Tremendous efforts are made to bring people to Christ but, having accepted him, they are given no idea as to what he expects of them from then on.

The Navigators, a Christian organisation which works mainly among students, has taken 2 Timothy 2:2 as its basic text for ministry. From this it has developed an excellent way of 'making disciples':

> 'And the things you have heard me say in the presence of many witnesses entrust to reliable men who will also be qualified to teach others.'

Navigators 'invest' their lives in others. Their goal is to spend quality time with a new Christian – perhaps for as long as five years – helping him or her learn about the faith and encouraging them to practice living it out.

INVEST IN PEOPLE

Using the gifts that God has given us will mean investing time, energy, prayer and love in the lives of people. That is how the church grows! Jesus invested three years of his life in a small group of twelve disciples. He showed them how to grow the gifts he had, teaching them how to pray and how to do the miracles he did; teaching them about God and how to live together as his followers. It was a practical, day-by-day apprenticeship; learning on the job.

Timothy's gifts were in teaching and preaching so Paul encouraged him to pass on the tools of the trade to other potential teachers and preachers. At root, this meant passing on to them the things Paul had taught him so that they in turn would be able to teach them to others. This happened in a dramatic way in the early life of the church: the twelve disciples became the one hundred and twenty; those in turn were joined by three thousand on the day of Pentecost, and so on down the generations until the church became worldwide.

As parents, teachers, work friends and neighbours we are called to invest our lives in others, perhaps moving them on a little nearer to faith or helping consolidate the faith they already have.

We spend a great amount of our time investing in things that are simply not going to last. They are trivial in comparison to investment in the things of the kingdom of God. It helps to remember that all our prized possessions will be dust in a hundred years time and our best achievements will have long since been forgotten! In the words of the old verse:

> 'We have only one life,
> It will soon be past.
> What's done for Christ
> Is all that will last.'

Invest in yourself

We can also make a direct investment in our own lives. In fact, it is vital that we do if we are to last any longer than Sandra did, because keeping up the Christian life is hard work. There are so many obstacles!

For one thing, the Bible is a difficult book to understand. It was first written in three languages, Hebrew, Aramaic and Greek, each of which is hard for the average twentieth-century reader to learn. But it is a book with which we are going to have to grapple. Sometimes people come to me and say, 'I'm having difficulty with reading the Bible.' I occasionally reach out and shake their hand. 'So am I!' The Bible won't reveal its treasures to the casual observer. It won't strengthen us at the deepest level if we simply flick through its pages, looking at the odd verse and hoping that something relevant will leap off the page at us. Sometimes God *does* speak to us in that way but the Bible yields its deepest treasure only to hard work, study and prayer.

Secondly, the church is hard work. To be honest, we don't always find it easy to maintain good relationships with others in our church:

'To fellowship above with saints we love,
Oh! That will be glory!
To fellowship below with saints we know,
Well – that's a different story!'

The church is hard work because it is made up of people like you and me! God has put us in a church family where we rub shoulders with real people, from different backgrounds to ourselves, with different upbringings, educational achievements, priorities and family circumstances. On top of these there are the simply 'prickly' who get offended at the drop of a hymn book!

Sometimes we turn the pages of the Old and

New Testaments and think, 'Look at these characters! If only we could be like them! If only we could be like Daniel or David!' As if they were absolutely perfect and didn't have family problems, corns and dandruff, as well as all the pressures of a world that didn't want anything to do with their faith! The reality is that wherever God's people are trying to live out their commitment to him, some hard work is called for. Paul wanted Timothy to be clear about that:

> 'Endure hardship with us like a good soldier of Christ Jesus. No-one serving as a soldier gets involved in civilian affairs – he wants to please his commanding officer. Similarly, if anyone competes as an athlete, he does not receive the victor's crown unless he competes according to the rules. The hardworking farmer should be the first to receive a share of the crops.'
> *2 Timothy 2:3–6*

Clear out the clutter!

When we recently moved house, my wife took it as an opportunity to throw out a lot of things we no longer needed – and a lot of things I thought we still did! The first I knew of this was when a friend came to see me one day, and was wearing my jacket! It happened to be the day after a sale at church where there had been a 'good as new' stall!

House moves really are good times to get rid of all the clutter we've been tripping over for the last few years. Jam jars, paper bags, bits of old car tyres, boxes of rusty staples – all go to the local dump or recycling centre. We feel that we want to clear out the rubbish from the old house, the old life, and make a new start in a new house. As the deadline approaches, panic sets in and some of the stuff we probably could use goes out too! Better to throw it out, we think, than not be ready when the removal people come!

If we are to live an effective Christian life, everything else must take second place to that goal. Anything that hinders us must be thrown out ruthlessly. The imagery Paul uses is that of the soldier, utterly dedicated to his job, his single goal being to carry out well the orders given by his superiors. If we are determined to make a success of our Christian lives, it may be that some unhelpful friendships and interests will have to go. There are many lonely and marginalised people who need our care and support instead. Some attitudes will need to be rethought as we struggle to allow the mind of Christ to develop in us. Some time may have to be reordered – perhaps we should cut down on the amount of time we spend in front of 'the box' and invest it instead in doing things with the family.

John Stott writes, 'Every Christian is in some degree a soldier of Christ, even if he is as timid as Timothy. For, whatever our temperament, we cannot avoid the Christian conflict. And if we are to be good soldiers of Jesus Christ, we must be dedicated to the battle, committing ourselves to a life of discipline and suffering, and avoiding whatever may 'entangle' us and so distract us from it.'[2]

Keep in shape!

Today's Olympic runner won't be awarded a gold medal – or even a bronze one – unless he competes according to the rules. Ben Johnson, for one, has found that out to his cost. In the Olympics of the first century AD there were similar rules about training and preparation for the games. Before he was permitted to enter the games, each athlete had to stand before a statue of Jupiter and swear, with one hand on his heart, that he had been in hard training for six months. If he could not swear that, he was automatically disqualified from taking part. The judges didn't want to waste their time watching a motley crowd of no-hopers!

Paul was impressed by the athletes' dedication. But even he was afraid that after having coached people for the olympic struggles of the Christian life he would himself be found out of shape, unfit to qualify for entry to the race.

It is vital that, as we use our gifts to help others live Christianly, we keep ourselves in shape spiritually. We need to develop a daily fitness programme that includes the press-ups of prayer, the body-building of Bible reading, and the weights of witnessing (not to mention the squat-thrusts of systematic attendance at

Sunday services)! Fighting the flab takes time, effort and a commitment of the will.

Stick at it!

Paul thinks of another analogy: the hard-working farmer. Even in these days of tractor cabs with built-in stereos and wall-to-wall carpeting, a farmer's work still demands daily perseverance. The cows have to be milked at five o'clock each morning, whether dawn breaks warm and clear or the sleet is hammering down on the window panes! The fields have to be ploughed and the crops sown and weeded if the arable farmer is to reap anything worth selling at the end of the season.

We need to be aware that Christianity is not a soft option. 'You don't need to tell *me* that!' may be your response! But sometimes we do present Christianity as the answer to every problem without understanding that the message of Timothy, as of the whole Bible, is that it involves commitment to a lifetime of hard work.

Many an elderly Christian will vouch that living out their faith doesn't get easier as time goes on. One member of our church, now in his seventies, has had to cope with enormous changes in church life alone! New people, new songs, new forms of worship – and that on top of coping with the gradual loss of physical freedom and the griefs of outliving longstanding friends.

But his verdict on all this? 'It's good to see God at work!'

That is good news! God *is* at work. We will be sustained and strengthened by him throughout our lives. It is his Holy Spirit working through us who ensures that what we do will be effective and fruitful. We need to hold these two facts in tension: praying as if the success of the ministries he has given us is all up to God, while working as if it is all up to us! Otherwise, we will find ourselves in one of two situations:

● Being too 'God-confident'. Some people over-emphasise the sovereignty of God in an almost fatalistic way and get bogged down in a porridge-like holy laziness. 'If God wants that to be done', they think, 'he will see that it is!' Then they hand back all responsibility to God and convince themselves that the truly spiritual thing to do is – nothing. This way of thinking provides one of the worst excuses for lazy Christianity I have ever heard!

● Being too self-confident. At the other end of the scale are Christians who are so self-confident that they don't take God's Spirit into account at all. They work hard at things but nothing of eternal significance happens because God is left out of the equation.

It is only when the two facts of God's sovereignty and

human responsibility are brought together that God's work gets done in God's way.

Relax! And trust God

The last letter John Wesley wrote before his death in 1791 was to William Wilberforce. Wilberforce had many gifts. He was deeply caring and was incensed at the way wealthy westerners were keeping the slave trade going. He was a thinking person and knew that slave trading was wrong. But he also had gifts of 'doing' and God called him to combine all three areas of gifting to launch a campaign against the slave trade. This was his ministry. Thinking about Wilberforce's campaign, John Wesley wrote:

> 'Unless God has raised you up for this very thing, you will be worn out by the opposition of men and devils. But if God be for you, who can be against you? Are all of them stronger than God? Oh be not weary of well-doing. Go on, in the name of God and in the power of his might, till even American slavery, the vilest thing that ever saw the sun, shall vanish away before it.'

Paul, like Wilberforce, knew what it was like to work so hard for years but feel he was getting nowhere. He knew the depths of despair and felt keenly the limitations of his humanity. But he had also found the key that unlocked the door of that cell:

> 'Remember Jesus Christ, raised from the dead, descended from David. This is my gospel, for which I am suffering even to the point of being chained like a criminal. But God's word is not chained. Therefore I endure everything for the sake of the elect, that they too may obtain the salvation that is in Christ Jesus, with eternal glory.'
>
> *2 Timothy 2:8–10*

When the going gets tough, he says, 'Remember Jesus Christ, raised from the dead, descended from David.' This statement flatly contradicted a heresy of the day which denied that Jesus was both God and man. In being 'raised from the dead' Jesus was proved to be God's Son; the phrase speaks of his divine nature. 'Descended from David' speaks of his human nature.

There are two things we need to grasp if we are to escape being paralysed emotionally by problems that hit us in our ministries. The first is that Jesus understands us! He knows just how we feel – he, too, had the onerous task of serving God as a mere human being. But, secondly, because Jesus is also God, he has the power to *do* something about our pain and suffering.

I think the three most devastating causes of self-doubt and despair that hit us as we try to use our God-given gifts are these.

● Criticism. There is the one-off, insensitive or spiteful remark: a young woman who has practised hard and struggled with nervousness in order to sing a solo at the evening service is greeted at the door afterwards with, 'You didn't sing very well tonight; what went wrong?' It takes immense courage and a mature assessment of one's abilities to be able to weather that and sing again.

Living with a constant undercurrent of criticism is perhaps even harder to cope with. The feeling that people are not approving of what you are doing can make you wary and unsure of yourself. A creeping 'paralysis' can take over as you double-check all your plans, so making you less effective in your ministry.

• Facing limitations. Secondly, sooner or later you make the discovery that you are not omnicompetent! It is hard to admit to having limitations. Physical energy, time, gifts can all be exhausted; there is a certain point beyond which you cannot go. It is sometimes painful to have to admit that someone else will have to do that particular job you always wanted to – and it can be stressful, too, if you think you could do it better!

• Lack of job satisfaction. Thirdly, particularly for those whose gifts are in caring for others, there is the lack of tangible job satisfaction. With any 'people-centred' work it is difficult to assess how you are doing. You can't be encouraged by the sales figures, take pride in the fact that the books balance, admire the finished car or wave goodbye to a satisfied client! The carer is always in a vulnerable position as far as job satisfaction is concerned.

All three debilitating factors can hit us particularly hard as we try to balance the demands of work, home and church. Criticism can come from all sides when one or another feels they are not getting a big enough slice of our time. We become painfully aware of our lack of ability to be in three places at once, and we're never quite sure we have done *any* of the jobs well!

When they join forces these three giants prove formidable foes – strong enough, it would seem, to put anyone's God-given ministry firmly under lock and key. If that is how you feel, Paul would sympathise. Writing to Timothy, he comments that his preaching of the gospel had led directly to his 'being chained like a criminal'. But he doesn't write himself into a depression; rather, he adds triumphantly, 'But God's word is not chained!'

Martin Luther, the sixteenth-century German reformer, was once taken into hiding, for his own safety, to an old, disused fortress. He was there for over a year. At the beginning of that time, away from all the action of reform happening in his home town, he became very anxious and depressed. Writing to a friend he poured out his frustration but the friend's reply helped restore Luther's sense of perspective: 'Look,

God's work is going on, Martin! You're not the only one doing it, you know!'

When the truth of this had sunk in, Luther wrote in his journal: 'While I sit here sipping my beer, the gospel runs its course.' He had got to the point of saying, 'Lord, I'm still asking you to get me out of this place but I praise you that, even while I'm stuck here, your work is getting done.'

From time to time we all need to be released from the pressure to be *achieving* something for God. We all go through periods of illness, hospitalisation or family pressure when we are simply unable to be what we want to be. We are unable to witness or share Christ with others as we would want to. It is then that we need to hear the Lord's reassurance: 'I love you and I know about the situation you are in, and I want to tell you that even while you feel unable to do anything, I'm still getting my work done. Relax!'

While Jan and I were on a recent sabbatical visit to Texas, Jan was taken ill and I drove her to the emergency department of the hospital for treatment. When we returned she went straight to bed feeling worse than before! She remained ill for the rest of our time there and by the time we had to leave she was feeling very frustrated. 'While I lay there,' she said, 'I kept thinking, what a waste of a sabbatical this is! I'm supposed to be doing things that are useful here!' She added, 'Even when I tried to pray for you and for all that was happening I just couldn't concentrate.'

But what kind of God do we serve? Was he standing there at Jan's bedside saying, 'You know, this is really pathetic! I mean, you have started this sentence *three times* now!' No, God isn't like that. He understood the situation. Jan's little bits of heartfelt groaning to God were just as acceptable to him as any well thought out, carefully constructed prayer. The *last* thing Jan needed was a heavy-handed pastoral visit: 'Have you had your devotions this morning? Why not? Where is the Bible? Pray, woman!'

There will be times when you are simply unable to use your gifts. God wants you to know that he loves you very much and that his word is not chained even when you are. God is big enough to cope with your situation and will handle his world and his business himself for the time being!

Invest in Christ

'Here is a trustworthy saying:
If we died with him,
we will also live with him;
If we endure,
we will also reign with him.
If we disown him,
he will also disown us;
if we are faithless,
he will remain faithful,

for he cannot disown himself.'
2 Timothy 2:11–13

Many people think these verses are part of a song that the early Christians sang. It could have been one of the first songs written for a 'Make Way' march or, at any rate, for an evangelistic presentation. Perhaps we should imagine Timothy at the head of a 'Make Way' procession, with his lyre or lute, leading the local Christians through the streets of their town declaring the good news of Jesus and singing the song, 'If we die with him we will also live with him.'

It was a challenge to the folk who heard it: 'You think you are living life now, but it is only when you have died to yourself that you will really live.' It speaks of the principle of giving all that we have and are into the hands of Jesus. The next phrase carries the same idea, 'If we endure, we will also reign with him.' It is an appeal to people, 'Come and die to yourself and live instead for Christ. And if you keep that commitment to him, you will find yourself reigning with him for ever.' What a great evangelistic message! 'Come and experience all the glory of the real kingdom!'

These verses are exceptionally difficult to understand though. The many commentaries on this passage all say different things. When we get to heaven we can ask Paul what he really meant! The difficulty lies with the phrase, 'If we disown him, he will disown us', because it seems, at first sight, to be a direct contradiction of what follows, 'If we are faithless, he will remain faithful, for he cannot disown himself.'

What Paul may be getting at is this. 'If we disown him' refers to something that has happened in the past. It was a one-off thing, a single event. If we, at one point, disowned him, 'he will also disown us'. Paul is probably remembering Jesus' words, 'Whoever acknowledges me before men, I will also acknowledge him before my Father in heaven. But whoever disowns me before men, I will disown him before my Father in heaven' (Matthew 10:32–33). If someone hears the message of Jesus and then says, 'I don't want anything to do with that, it's not for me,' God, in his infinite mercy and love, says, 'Fine, if you don't want me, I can't have you.' In that moment that person disowns Christ and is disowned by God. There can be no other outcome. God has given us the gift of free will and it is only as we exercise that free will that he can offer us his gift of salvation. If we say we do not want anything to do with his way, he will disown us. He is bound to.

This is a reminder we urgently need today. Many people seem to think that 'everyone will get there in the end'. It doesn't matter what you believe or don't believe, or what you commit yourself to or do not; God loves us so much, they say, that he will see we're all right in the end. But that is an outright denial of human liberty! If we disown God, he will take our decision *seriously* and will not overrule it. He will not make us *less* than human.

Paul goes on to hammer the nail into the coffin. 'If we are faithless, he will remain faithful, for he cannot disown himself.'

'If we are faithless' indicates *going on* being. It is not referring to a single event in the past. If we continue to be faithless, we not only disown Christ once but reject the gospel message time and again. If we keep on refusing to have anything to do with him, 'he will remain faithful'. What does that mean? It does not mean that he will eventually say, 'All right, I know that you keep on rejecting me, but I've run out of patience and I'm going to accept you now despite your rejection.' It means, rather, that God is faithful to his original word, which was, 'he will also disown us.' So, if we continue to be faithless God will be faithful to himself and, being faithful to himself, will continue to disown us. That is why these verses have such a powerful evangelistic thrust.

We can be equally sure, however, that if we come to God, in faith, God will instantly cancel all our past rejection of him and say, 'Thank goodness for that! I own you. I love you. I want you and I will keep you for ever in my grasp.'

So, while these verses look forbidding in one sense, they

contain a message of hope. They show that God is just, righteous and reliable and does not change his mind about things halfway through. We would never know where we stood with him if he did.

All this means that we are thoroughly wise to invest our lives, gifts and all our energies in serving Jesus. No fears here of a 'Black Monday' crash and of losing all our assets! Investment in serving Christ is costly and demanding but gilt-edged security is guaranteed. Christians intent on growing their gifts should invest in nothing but the best!

4
GROWING CHRISTIAN CHARACTER

'Building character' sounds a bit old-fashioned, straight-backed and army-like today, but it is still a crucial part of the Christian life. God is vitally concerned about who we *become* in the course of our lives – just as much as he is about what we *do* in life. This is because, in a real sense, 'character is destiny'. Who we are, in terms of character, will affect what we accomplish. We can have every gift going, but if our characters are not becoming increasingly Christlike we will not be able to use those gifts effectively for him.

In practical terms, Paul pinpoints three aspects of character that should be apparent in our lives: integrity in handling the Bible, holy living, and a servant attitude. He weaves together teaching on all three in his letter to Timothy, showing how each is vital to the other two and how each undergirds and makes possible the others.

INTEGRITY IN HANDLING THE BIBLE

> 'Do your best to present yourself to God as one approved, a workman who does not need to be ashamed and who correctly handles the word of truth.'
> *2 Timothy 2:15*
> '. . . from infancy you have known the holy Scriptures, which are able to make you wise for salvation through faith in Christ Jesus. All Scripture is God-breathed and is useful for teaching, rebuking, correcting and training in righteousness, so that the man of God may be thoroughly equipped for every good work.'
> *2 Timothy 3:15–17*

It is very easy to twist – ever so slightly – what someone has said, so that it puts us in a better light. We 'reinterpret' a statement until we are happy with what we have made it say: 'Well, I know double yellow lines mean "No parking", but I'm not really *parking* here – just stopping for a couple of minutes to get to the bank!' The ticket on your windscreen when you get back will suggest that you and the traffic warden differ over your definitions of 'parking'!

Though we admit to being a bit free with our interpretation of the comments and rules we come across each day, we need to treat the Bible with respect. When we offer advice and teaching to others, we must be sure that we are really passing on the mind of God, not simply giving the thoughts that we or our hearers find most acceptable. So we need to understand what the Bible is teaching and we need to bring our own lives into line with what it says.

Understanding the Bible

The Bible is no mere human invention; it is not just the product of forty clever minds writing sixty-six books over a span of nearly two thousand years, but the product of the mind of God. In that case, how can we be expected to understand it?

Firstly, God used ordinary people to write the Bible – it is presented in normal, human languages and in concepts that can be grasped by anyone familiar with those languages. We are not all accomplished readers of Greek, Hebrew and Aramaic, however! So, secondly, we have translations and books of explanation written by those who are. There are also countless commentaries on individual books of the Bible. Many of these are designed to help the ordinary Christian learn how to handle the Bible and apply its teaching with integrity. If you are in a position of church leadership, perhaps as an elder or housegroup leader, you should be building up a library of such books to help you as you teach others.[3]

Handling the Bible with integrity means taking all of it seriously – Old Testament as well as New. We tend to make a big distinction between the two, thinking that the New Testament is 'interesting' and 'all about good things', whereas the Old Testament is 'difficult' and 'some day I'll get round to looking at it!' Gordon MacDonald, the author of *Ordering your private world* and *Restoring your spiritual passion*, suggests that we think of the Old Testament as 'the older Testament', to help us see it in its true light. It is not like an old vacuum cleaner that we throw out once we've got a new one; it's more like the first volume of a two-book novel. We won't understand what's really happening in the second one until we know what happened earlier.

The picture of God that we have from the Old Testament is always in the background of what we read of him in the New. The Old Testament gives us clues about the nature of God and how he related to people in large groups, particularly nations. It shows his concern for their laws and general principles of social justice. It is also the canvas on which the New Testament picture of Jesus is painted; without the canvas, there is no picture. The New Testament unfolds the reasons why God became man in Jesus and shows how we can have access not just to a fuller understanding of God but can come right into his presence.

'Doing' the Bible

As Christians we recognise that God's word has authority over us: we will let it step into our lives and change the way we live. God's word comes to us most clearly in the Bible, and we can have every confidence in the Bible's truth. It describes itself as 'God-breathed'. That is, it comes straight from the heart of God and when you read it you recognise the Spirit that breathed it. *Mein Kampf* breathes the spirit of its author, Adolf Hitler. It simply reeks of his megalomania. You cannot read the book without knowing something about the man, even though he is not writing directly about himself. You cannot read *Das Kapital* without understanding something of the sort of person that Karl Marx was; it breathes out his personality. Neither can you read the Bible honestly without knowing that it breathes out a unique personality beyond those of its human authors – Peter, Paul, Isaiah, Jeremiah and others. It is because the Bible is God-breathed that it is authoritative.

We will not find God in his fullness nor know how to use our gifts fully in his service until his word is authoritative in our lives. We are far more comfortable when we sit in judgement over the Bible, trying to keep some measure of control over it: 'Well, I quite like that bit but not that,' and 'I don't think that bit applies to me but maybe this does.' Others would not claim to sit 'above' the Bible but think it is important to sit 'around' it, like nothing more than a discussion group, talking about it with other folk, seeing who can convince whom of their particular viewpoint. The only way we will find out what it is that God wants us to be and do is to sit 'under' the Bible's authority, accepting and obeying its teaching.

Many new Christians, and people thinking about

becoming Christians, are sceptical about the Bible. They feel they need to give it time to 'prove' itself. 'I'm an intelligent person and I'm not going to believe a word of this Bible until I can see some reason to. Why should I take any notice of what uneducated, superstitious people thought in the first century?'

One Saturday morning you are walking along the street when you come across two people in their front drives, each with a car Repair Manual, a broken-down car, and no idea how to mend it. One of them picks up the Manual and says, 'I'm not stupid. I'm just as intelligent as the person who wrote this Manual. How do I know if he's got it right? I think I'll check every single one of his instructions. In fact, at different points, I think I'll do things differently to the way he suggests because he may not have got it right at all.' For each instruction in the book, this person asks, 'How do I know *that* instruction is right?' Or says, 'That doesn't make much sense to me; I'll miss out that step.'

The other person takes the Manual, props it up against the garage wall and reads, '*Step one*: open Manual (you must already have done this.)' '*Step two*: the thing with four wheels is a car.' '*Step three*: open the front bit.' And so on. He just follows the instructions, one after the other. He has no idea whether the person who wrote the Manual is right or not but neither does he know how to mend a car! So he simply follows the instructions and gets his car back on the road long before the other guy!

Some people are very cynical about the Bible. They are bright and wonderfully sophisticated people but their lives go on rusting by the side of the road because they will not allow the 'Repair Manual' to sort them out. They would rather let the car stay off the road than trust themselves to what someone else says.

It is important not to ignore the questions that arise in our minds about the Bible, but it is important to put aside our cynicism. If the Bible *is* true, what it says will work and will make a difference to our lives. But we will discover whether or not it is true only if we take the risk of following its instructions.

Paul doesn't leave us simply with the assurance that the Bible is authoritative and totally trustworthy. He goes on to explain exactly how it is that the Bible helps us live Christianly.

Firstly, it 'rebukes' us. As we read it and open ourselves to the prompting of the Holy Spirit, we become aware of where we are falling short of God's standards. We invite the Holy Spirit to step in and point out where and how we need to change.

Secondly, it 'corrects' us: it brings us back onto the right track. The tense of the verb, 'correcting', is present continuous; the Bible keeps on correcting our way. Many young people today are subjected to orthodontic work, having a brace fitted to crooked teeth to pull them back into line. It's usually a long process. The orthodontist doesn't fit the brace one afternoon and say, 'There, take that off in the morning and you'll be all straightened out!' The brace works on the principle that it keeps on working. Over a period of time it pulls the teeth back into line. Our behaviour is not corrected simply by hearing once what God has to say about it. Rather, as we continually hear him, his Spirit continually helps us adjust.

Thirdly, Paul emphasises that if we understand the Bible and do what it says we will be 'fully equipped for every good work' of Christian ministry.

When I first witnessed American football and saw all the gear they wear, I was fascinated. They are swathed in protective gear including helmets and huge shoulder pads. It makes you wonder whether the nine-foot high giants who come out onto the pitch are actually only three-foot-six midgets underneath all their padding! Imagine these modern-day knights in all their armour being joined on the field by an Englishman thinking he was going to play rugby, and had dressed accordingly. We are talking painful!

You and I need to be equipped for the battles of ministering in Christ's name, armoured and suited up. The only way we are going to be ready to face the hassles and aggro, pressure and pain, is to be equipped by the Bible. Those who neglect it, both in its preaching and teaching and in its private reading, are going to be defenceless when exposed to the problems of the world. Spiritual injury is the inevitable result.

HOLY LIVING

The goal of the Christian life is righteous, holy living. Vance Havner, an American preacher, once said, 'If you want to be popular, preach happiness. If you want to be unpopular, preach holiness.'

Of course, happiness and holiness are not necessarily mutually exclusive! We sometimes have odd views, though, of what holiness is. We expect a holy person to radiate a sort of luminosity and always wear a serene, Mona Lisa smile. But real holiness is something very earthy and practical. It will affect the things we say and do, but above all it will affect the way we relate to other people.

In writing to Timothy, Paul speaks of a gentle and humble spirit as one of the main characteristics of a holy life:

'Keep reminding them of these things. Warn them before God against quarrelling about words; it is of no value, and only ruins those who listen. . . Avoid godless chatter because those who indulge in it will become more and more ungodly. Their teaching will spread like gangrene. Among them are Hymenaeus and Philetus, who have wandered away from the truth. They say that the resurrection has already taken place, and they destroy the faith of some.

Don't have anything to do with foolish and stupid arguments, because you know they produce quarrels. And the Lord's servant must not quarrel; instead, he must be kind to everyone, able to teach, not resentful. Those who oppose him he must gently instruct, in the hope that God will grant them repentance leading them to a knowledge of the truth, and that they will come to their senses and escape from the trap of the devil, who has taken them captive to do his will.'

2 Timothy 2:14–26

Sometimes we come across Christians who simply cannot discuss a point of conflict with humility, gentleness and love.

There was once a preacher, a Baptist and a staunch Baptist at that. No other denomination was really *Christian*, in his view. If you weren't a Baptist – well, you were just the pits! He went to preach at a church that was preparing to take part in a week of prayer for Christian unity. At the end of the meeting he asked,

'How many people in this church are Baptist?'

It was a Baptist church and, knowing his reputation, almost all the local non-Baptists had stayed away. So nearly everyone in the congregation put up their hands – all except one little old lady.

The preacher decided to embarrass her. He told the others to put their hands down and he said to her,

'What denomination are you?'

'I'm a Methodist', she replied.

'A *what*?'

'A Methodist,' she said.

'And *why* are you a Methodist?' he asked.

'Well,' she said, 'my father was a Methodist and my grandfather was a Methodist, so I'm a Methodist.'

The preacher decided that he would really make his point here, so he said,

'That's simply ridiculous! Suppose your father was a moron and your grandfather was a moron, what would *that* make you?'

The little old lady thought for a moment, then replied, 'I guess that would make me a Baptist!'

Sometimes there is an unhealthy arrogance about us. It is right to be confident about what the Bible teaches but we can become very conceited about our own interpretations of it. This shows itself particularly in personal conversation with other Christians. I have heard people from different churches getting together in a corner after joint events and arguing hammer and tongs about which one of them is right. Each says, 'But it says *this* in the Bible!' And the 'discussion' ends up as a heated slagging match: 'You feel free *not* to believe the Bible then!'

This is not warm, open discussion. Nor is it helpful to anyone. God calls us to a new humility and gentleness in our personal relationships. The bold proclamation of God's word is essential and the strongest authoritative teaching is crucial. But when people are hungry for the truth, or searching or disagreeing, the time for arguing is over. In private, personal relationships with other believers and with non-Christians, we need the spirit Timothy had – one of confidence in the Bible but also of humility and a lack of arrogance.

Holiness is a bit like measles: it's catching. But so is unholiness. When we are away from strong Christian fellowship, our fellowship with God grows weak. It is easy for our language to become displeasing to him. It is also easier to hang loose to the truth of the gospel and so undermine the faith of others.

Paul warned Timothy about two types of people. The first are characterised by Hymenaeus and Philetus. Their talking had affected their thinking and then their teaching, so that they had ended up destroying the faith of some believers. People like this know in their hearts that Jesus is Saviour, but are wilfully and deliberately sinning. Those folk will not be brought back to the kingdom of God by Bible-bashing, anger or rebuke, but only by love.

The other group of people Paul describes are those who have never found Jesus for themselves as

Saviour and Lord. They, too, are going to be won to him only by the quiet, gentle and humble spirit of men and women of God who are so certain of their ground that they don't need to shout or be abrasive or angry, but can present the gospel lovingly and clearly. In our own day, many have found this true of Billy Graham's preaching. The simplicity of the gospel message he presents, combined with his certainty, gentleness and lack of pressurised 'hype', breaks down many barriers to faith.

A SERVANT ATTITUDE

> 'In a large house there are articles not only of gold and silver, but also of wood and clay; some are for noble purposes and some for ignoble. If a man cleanses himself from the latter, he will be an instrument for noble purposes, made holy, useful to the Master and prepared to do any good work.'
>
> *2 Timothy 2:20–21*

Not everything that glitters in the church is necessarily gold – and that goes for the people too! Characters like Hymenaeus and Philetus seem to be really useful to begin with but their true colours soon show. Paul describes these people as 'ignoble', that is, unfit for use in God's work. We cannot always spot people like this, but God can! He won't use, for any of his 'noble' purposes, people who deliberately deviate from his word. We need to work hard to keep close to God, living in obedience to him. When we do this our gifts can be used by God with all the honour reserved for the best china – which is the marvellous alternative to being treated like a polystyrene cup!

The reward for holiness in our lives is service and not status. Being spiritually clean will make us '*useful* to the Master and prepared *to do any good work*'! William Barclay, commenting on these verses, challenges our motives and calls us to selfless ministry:

> 'A really good man does not regard his goodness as entitling him to special honour . . . His glory will not be in exemption from service; it will be in still more demanding service. No Christian should ever think of fitting himself for honour but always as fitting himself for service.'[4]

In practice, there are some steps we can take to help develop this attitude.

• Firstly, remember that it is not ability but availability that matters. Just because God chooses us to be his ministers in a certain place it doesn't mean that we are anything very special. After all, he has spoken through a donkey before now (Numbers 22:21–34)! The sovereign of the universe chooses us for *his* reasons, not for who we are. God does not use us because we are specially able but because we make ourselves totally available to him.

● Secondly, remember that *our* accomplishments count for nothing; only those things done by God's Spirit will have enduring worth. The prophet Zechariah reminded King Zerubbabel of this at the same time as he encouraged him in his work of rebuilding the temple: 'Not by might nor by power, but by my Spirit, says the Lord Almighty' (Zechariah 4:6).

● Thirdly, remember that true Christian service springs from love. If we serve God from any motive other than love we will only be harming ourselves and those around us. If we are honest, we have to admit that much of our Christian service is done because we feel we have to. It may be that we think it is expected of us and that we won't be thought to be 'pulling our weight' in the church if we don't. Or we may not be secure enough in God's love. Deep down we feel that he won't *really* accept us unless we are running a weekly house group, transporting old ladies to and from the Women's Fellowship, preaching at least once a month, teaching Sunday School, witnessing to our neighbours *and* going to six services every Sunday. But God doesn't need his arm twisted in order to love us. He demonstrated his unfathomable love for us long before we were in existence, let alone doing anything for him. All he wants from us in return is our love. True service will grow out of that.

5

STRENGTH
FOR
TOUGH TIMES

If you have spent much time in Christian book shops, you will know that there are almost as many theories about the second coming as there are Christians! There are pre-millennialists, post-millennialists and a-millennialists.[5] There are those who believe the church will go through a time of intense tribulation before Jesus comes back and those who think Christians will be taken to be with Christ in the middle of those tribulations or a little later on, or at the end. It's all very confusing. I'm a 'pan-millennialist': I believe it will all pan out in the end!

While the Bible does not set out to give us a timetable, it is very clear about two things: firstly, 'the last days' are here. Secondly, they will, in places, be 'terrible'. They are 'the tough times' and Paul warns Timothy to be ready for them:

'There will be terrible times in the last days. People will be lovers of themselves, lovers of money, boastful, proud, abusive, disobedient to their parents, ungrateful, unholy, without love, unforgiving, slanderous, without self-control, brutal, not lovers of the good, treacherous, rash, conceited, lovers of pleasure rather than lovers of God – having a form of godliness but denying its power. Have nothing to do with them.

They are the kind who worm their way into homes and gain control over weak-willed women, who are loaded down with sins and are swayed by all kinds of evil desires, always learning but never being able to acknowledge the truth. Just as Jannes and Jambres opposed Moses, so also these men oppose the truth – men of depraved minds, who, as far as the faith is concerned, are rejected. But they will not get very far because, as in the case of those men, their folly will be clear to everyone.'

2 Timothy 3:1–9

The Jews of Paul's day divided history into two parts, current time and 'the last days'. The New Testament writers use the phrase, 'the last days', to mean the entire period after the death and resurrection of Jesus, up until his second coming. In the New Testament, the crucial words linked with the second coming are 'soon!' and 'be ready!' Whenever the apostles were asked about the second coming they said, 'The Lord is coming soon', emphasising the need to be ready. The importance of that was stressed by Jesus himself. He warned his disciples to keep awake and alert, just as they would be at three o'clock in the morning if they'd had a tip-off about being burgled! (See Luke 12:35–40.)

But why should this time be particularly difficult for Christians? Paul mentions two pressures that we will feel and gives some hints on how to cope with them.

PRESSURE FROM SOCIETY

The first pressure has two aspects. Society at large is going to be hostile towards the Christian faith; being different is going to be a real struggle. But at the same time God is wanting to change our characters so that we become more Christlike. As he does that, we will find ourselves swimming more obviously against the tide. Let's look at some of the characteristics of society which Paul highlights as hostile to Christian faith.

Personal qualities

'People will be . . . boastful, proud . . .' There is some difference between the two. One evening some years ago I played football at Luton Town Football Club. As I ran out onto the artificial pitch the crowds cheered. All the old magic returned. The crowds gasped at the ability of this centre-forward, thinking, 'Why isn't he playing full-time – a man with this kind of skill?' Then, at the end, three laps of honour and back to the dressing room.

Now, there is only one element in that account which is true: I did play football at Luton Town Football Club but the rest is pure embroidery to make a good story. I actually felt sick after the first two minutes! Most of us are experts at dressing up a simple incident – something we did or that happened to us – in order to impress other people. You know the sort of thing: 'I had lunch with so-and-so today, the *very famous person* (along with – ahem – three thousand other people).' We try to make ourselves look good in other people's eyes. That is what 'boastful' means.

Pride is something more sinister because it is an inner attitude. Most of the time other people can tell what we are really like – they know when we are boasting! Pride is much harder to detect. It sometimes comes across as cynicism. We may not brag or boast about anything but inside we consider ourselves 'superior' to other people. We look down our noses at them, firmly believing that we are better than they are because of our intellect or because we are more spiritual or understand the Bible better.

Pride is a deadly disease in the church. It comes across in the way we can almost casually dismiss someone else. It can only be fought with constant vigilance, by regularly examining our attitudes or by giving a very honest friend permission to pull us up when he or she can see us slipping.

'People will be . . . abusive, disobedient to their parents, ungrateful.' Ungratefulness is a hallmark of our society. 'Demand your rights,' is the slogan of the day. We have a terrible inability to say 'thank you' and to be gracious in thanking others for what they do for us. That applies in our church life too: we find it hard to praise, thank and worship God for all that he has done for us. If we organise a time to intercede for someone, many people may turn up and pray with passion. That's good! But if we hold a prayer time just to say, 'thank you' to God and to praise him for what he has done, it could easily be the flattest and most difficult prayer time ever! Let's pray for the gift of gratitude.

'People will be . . . unholy, without love, unforgiving, slanderous' – and when they are they will be thought of as witty, especially if they're writing in a satirical magazine! This sort of attitude is institutionalised in segments of our society, perhaps most obviously in the popular press where sales depend on sensationalism and 'shock reports'.

The word translated 'slanderous' is more often translated 'devilish'. The powers of the tongue and pen are devilish when they tear down others. It is so easy to criticise others, so hard to build them up. Building people up seems to be of no advantage to ourselves, whereas taking them down a peg shows us off, we think, in a comparatively better light. Yet when we withhold praise, and destroy a person's character instead, we are letting our tongues be instruments of Satan and not of God. A simple 'thank you', a telephone call offering help or expressing appreciation, even remembering someone's name – all these are positive up-building uses of our tongue.

'If you drop that glove once more, I'll throw you down those stairs!' That was how one young mother communicated with her shivering two-year-old at the top of a flight of concrete steps leading out of a London underground station. *'People will be . . . without self-control, brutal.'*

Even our humour gets more crude and brutal. You can learn a great deal about a society by observing its humour, just as you know more about someone from what they laugh at than from almost anything else. Many of the things ordinary people in Britain hold dear are now the targets of cynical and manipulative TV comedians. As Christians we need to be careful that we do not allow these attitudes to others to take hold of us.

'People will be . . . not lovers of the good, treacherous, rash, conceited, lovers of pleasure, rather than lovers of God – having a form of godliness but denying its power'. The word translated 'form' is an interesting one. It means a 'model' and implies that a person can 'make a model' of godliness.

Madam Tussaud's in London is always worth a visit. Have you ever tried sitting very still on one of the seats they provide round the sides of the rooms? You know what happens: people wander past you and then they step back and take another look! A friend of mine tried this once. He sat very still in a thoughtful pose for quite some time, until an older lady came along with a friend. She looked at him for a while. Then she turned to her friend and said, 'This one's not very good.' She was startled and rather embarrassed when 'it' moved!

All the actors, presidents and politicians at Madam Tussauds are only 'forms' of someone. Some of them are exceptionally lifelike but they do not live. They could fool you in the half-light or at a distance but they're not real.

The culture of Victorian England had a 'form of godliness' but lacked its life and power. People went to church because their bosses did or because it was what made them culturally acceptable – but there was no life in their religious experience. Today in America, particularly in the Southern States, being a Christian can have the same air about it. Many people who go to church on a Sunday morning seem to do so with no real faith but because it is part of their culture.

It can happen to us, too. We can become 'Madame Tussaud Christians', sitting in church, saying all the right things, being part of the church family and even being heavily involved in its life – but being totally ineffective. We can perform the functions without allowing the Spirit of God to transform what we do into a reality that lasts. God wants us to have a real and satisfying faith. He is not interested in 'appearances'.

Public witness

Swimming against the tide of our culture doesn't stop with our private lives. Following Christ and using our gifts in his name is a very public business.

Some time ago I was talking with a BBC television commentator about Christian influence in the media. He said to me, 'While you were away in America, we heard a Chief of Police here talking about homosexuality and the AIDS issue, and saw him pilloried by every newspaper in the country, by TV, radio and by lots of very learned bishops and clergy. They were all outraged by any suggestions that AIDS might have anything to do with judgement and were saying, "We need to be very careful before we condemn homosexual practices." I looked in vain,' he said, 'for a Christian leader who was prepared to stand up on national television or say on the radio or in the press, "God has his standards and they will not be flouted." ' There is a time to use our gifts for 'thinking and talking' in the public arena.

On 22 November 1963, two great men died. One of them was assassinated in Dallas, Texas; the other died peacefully at home in Oxford, England. John Kennedy and C S Lewis both had a massive influence on our world but in quite different ways. Take C S Lewis, the author-theologian. In the academic environment of Oxford University he said that the Bible was the word of God and that full-blooded Christianity was true. And they laughed at him. In the 1940s, 1950s and 1960s you were not popular in academic institutions if you had a committed faith in God. Lewis stood alone in an environment that thought his beliefs had gone out with the Ark.

You also may have to stand alone as a Christian in your place of work, or perhaps you are the only Christian in your family. It may be that your actions or what you say will mark you out as being different. Through prayer and the support of other Christians, God wants to give you special grace for that situation. He loves you and does not want you to be afraid or to shy away from the cost involved in taking that stand for him.

There are times when even the strongest Christian feels shaken, unsure of himself and of God. At times like this it is good to remember three things:

• Your conversion. Think back to the time when Jesus Christ came into your life or first became real to you. He has promised that, once we are his, no-one and nothing can pluck us out of his hand: 'My sheep listen to my voice; I know them, and they follow me. I give them eternal life, and they shall never perish; no-one can snatch them out of my hand' (John 10:27–28). You can be sure that he has not let go of you, and will never do so! Relax in the security of this.

● Your call. Your call to use your gifts to serve God in a particular way, came with an inner sense that you were doing the right thing. And this was confirmed by others in the church, either 'officially' at a commissioning ceremony, or simply by their comments that you had a gift in that particular area. Now that you have pushed out the boat and begun to exercise that ministry, don't let the descending fog fool you into thinking it was all a mistake. Once you have set your course, you will need courage and determination to keep going in it, especially when you can't see any land ahead!

● Your commitment. In a world which lives for the good times and goes for immediate rewards, our ministries can soon end up in the cupboard along with the skate board and the Rubick cube. But things of significance are only achieved with time and commitment.

Paul appeals to Timothy to swim against the tide of his culture. 'But as for you, continue in what you have learned' (3:14). It is vital that, if our ministries are to be effective, we determine to follow and serve God as closely as we can, regardless of what anyone else is doing. Joshua threw down the same challenge to the people of Israel in the Old Testament: 'Choose for yourselves this day whom you will serve . . . but as for me and my household, we will serve the Lord.' (Joshua 24:15.)

OUTRIGHT OPPOSITION

The prevailing attitude of our culture, along with the painful changes God wants to make to our characters, will make 'the last days' tough. But there will also be outright, open opposition.

Preachers are often tempted to be dishonest in their proclamation of the gospel. 'Come to know Jesus,' they say, 'and life will be great! Wonderful! Marvellous! It's the best thing that can happen to you!' All of that is true, but we do not often give prospective converts the other side of the picture: 'Everyone who wants to live a godly life in Christ Jesus will be persecuted' (3:12).

Who by? Well, Satan to start with. He is pretty mad when someone becomes a Christian. Though you may not even know of his existence beforehand, when you become a Christian you soon find out about it! He works to prevent God's people from being effective, by getting at them through two routes: other Christians and the hostility of people outside the church.

Opposition from fellow Christians

The history of the church is full of examples of Christians disagreeing with each other to the point of withdrawing from fellowship. This is how most of our denominations have come into existence! It can be devastating to find that, on top of this, one's name is being tarred and feathered by those with whom one disagrees. It seems inevitable that any ministry will be damaged by this. Yet it does not always follow. John Wesley, the great eighteenth-century preacher who began Methodism, was always concerned to stay within the Anglican church, reforming from within. But many ministers barred him from their pulpits so he was forced to preach out of doors. Because of this, many thousands of people who would never have set foot inside a church heard the gospel and responded to it eagerly.

Paul warned Timothy to expect opposition to his ministry from within the church. It comes in many different forms. Sometimes there is stubborn opposition to the things of God. More often, opposition comes unwittingly from those who have forgotten Jesus' model of self-giving service and have taken on the models of the business world instead. Gifts can become fossilised until all that a person is doing is holding on to a position of power and prestige. Deacons can become dominated by traditionalism; youth workers start empire-building; house group leaders become motivated by pride not by love; PCC members make decisions about the church's future ministry on financial considerations alone and not on the basis of Spirit-directed insight.

In his imprisonment, suffering because of the gospel he had preached, Paul soon discovered who was genuine in their concern to serve God and who wasn't:

> 'You know that everyone in the province of Asia has deserted me, including Phygelus and Hermogenes.
> May the Lord show mercy to the household of Onesiphorus, because he often refreshed me and was not ashamed of my chains. On the contrary, when he was in Rome, he searched hard for me until he found me. May the Lord grant that he will find mercy from the Lord on that day! You know very well in how many ways he helped me in Ephesus.
> You then, my son, be strong in the grace that is in Christ Jesus.'   *2 Timothy 1:15–2:1*

It seems that Paul had called Phygelus and Hermogenes to work alongside him as trainees. Things appear to have started off well but very quickly they spotted that there was an angle of the gospel that could be exploited. Being in on the healings and miracles and seeing the way people were listening to the new teachings gave them a sense of power. What they needed in order to acquire that power for themselves was a slightly different version of the gospel, so they began to twist the message a little. When Paul tried to bring them back into line, he was not able to.

They distanced themselves more and more from Paul until they heard that he was in prison. Being connected with him then was anything but good for their image! They were ashamed to be associated with him. Although he had been their mentor, 'setting them up in business' and teaching them all he knew, they decided to have nothing more to do with him, his ministry or his name. But they went on manipulating and abusing the gospel for their own ends. Jesus denounced the Pharisees in strong terms for doing just this: 'You clean the outside of the cup and dish, but inside they are full of greed and self-indulgence . . . You are like whitewashed tombs, which look beautiful on the outside but on the inside are full of dead men's bones.' (Matthew 23:25, 27.)

As we take on different sorts of ministry within the church fellowship we will discover that some people are supporting us only for their own ends and will be ready to dump us at the slightest hint of trouble. There were plenty of people who said to Paul, 'Thank you *so much* for your great sermon! What a *terrific* crusade you led when you came to Smyrna! What a *wonderful* preacher! We will *never* forget your ministry; thank you for all you gave us!' Six months later Paul is alone, rotting in a Roman jail. 'There you are,' says Paul. 'What kind of friends were they, really?'

Loss of support from fellow Christians can take a heavy emotional toll. The biggest knocks, however, may come from outside the church.

Opposition from outside the church

I sometimes wonder if I have really understood what 'being a Christian' is all about. I wonder how much opposition you and I face because of our service to Christ. It's not that we don't suffer at all – we all have toothache and family problems and our water pipes burst when it snows – the sort of suffering everyone else has. But what about suffering for Christ's sake?

I do not believe we should *look* for opposition, but it seems that Paul saw that Christian service was so revolutionary that it would involve a particular kind of suffering and pressure:

> 'So do not be ashamed to testify about our Lord, or ashamed of me his prisoner. But join with me in suffering for the gospel, by the power of God, who has saved us and called us to a holy life – not because of anything we have done but because of his own purpose and grace. This grace was given us in Christ Jesus before the beginning of time, but it has now been revealed through the appearing of our Saviour, Christ Jesus, who has destroyed death and has brought life and immortality to light through the gospel. And of this gospel I was appointed a herald and an apostle and a teacher. That is why I am suffering as I am.

> Yet I am not ashamed, because I know whom I have believed, and am convinced that he is able to guard what I have entrusted to him for that day.'
> 2 Timothy 1:8–12

For Paul, opposition came as a direct result of his preaching ministry and he ended up in chains in a Roman jail. How did he cope with that, and how should we cope with the opposition that comes our way?

● Remember the eternal time-scale. Paul had no doubts that all his suffering was worthwhile. He measured its worth on a longer time-scale than those around him: 'I . . . am convinced that he is able to guard what I have entrusted to him for that day.'

The word Paul used for 'entrust' was a banking term meaning 'to place on deposit'. He was convinced that nothing could rob him of the benefits of his faith. Life here and now was being made pretty unpleasant for Paul and many people must have wondered what on earth he was getting out of his faith. To the pagan in the street it must have looked as though Paul was losing out in every way – and should be ashamed of his losses. But Paul lived by the principle that 'you get what you pay for'. A person who buys a Rembrandt print from a High Street department store won't get more than a few pence for it at a jumble sale in a year or two's time. But a collector who spends all he has on the original work will find his sacrifice repaid many times over at a future international auction!

In his first letter to the Christians at Corinth Paul freely admitted that if he was looking for a return for his faith in this life he was backing a loser: 'If only for this life we have hope in Christ, we are to be pitied more than all men' (1 Corinthians 15:19). But, he said, faith in Christ didn't work like that. It was as though he had placed his faith on deposit in God's bank vault where it was not just being kept safe but compounding interest. Though the benefits of it might not be seen straight away, on the day of Christ's return his deposit would be given back to him with interest which is out of this world! Ministry in his name is never wasted.

● Trust God. God promises that we can trust our future to him. If we have given our lives to Jesus Christ nothing can take away our security. No problem in our lives, no disaster, failure or world catastrophe will be able to rob us of the eternal benefits of our faith. God will guard what we have committed to him and no bank robber can get past him! We need to be honest about where our security lies. Is it really with God and with his people? If we find that we are actually more concerned about losing favour and prestige in the world we need to re-establish a solid centre of security that will last into eternity.

● Go on the attack! Don't be forced onto the defensive! There is no need to be a doormat or to give a milk-and-water impression of Christianity to your work colleagues. I have often been challenged to explain why there is suffering in the world – and given about two minutes to do so! I sometimes turn the question back on the questioners: 'First I'll give *you* two minutes to explain why there is suffering in the world!' Needless to say, they usually cannot. We don't know all the answers to the problems people face day by day, but those who reject Christian faith do not usually have better ideas of their own!

• Gather support. When you are aware of opposition building up, share your concerns with friends and with others involved in the same sort of ministry as yourself. Ask them to pray with you and pledge yourself to supporting them, too.

So Paul encourages Timothy to be reckless for the sake of the gospel – to stick his neck out to the extent of suffering for it. He was to regard opposition to Christian service as something normal and to be expected. The good news for the Christian is that we can stand firm in the face of set-backs and say, 'Thank you, Lord, that in the middle of this swirling storm of problems, there is rock-hard certainty: I have trusted all my life to you and I know that you will not let me down. Ultimately, I will find that you have kept me and have completed through me the work that you ask me to do.'

6

THE ART
OF
FRIENDSHIP

There are times when everything seems to conspire against you. Grandma had come to stay with us for a few days but no sooner had she arrived than our oldest daughter went down with a stomach bug. The next day my wife, Jan, went down with it too – not a very cheery welcome for Grandma. But someone in the church found out what had happened. Next day, she was round at our house sorting everything out: organising the children, looking after Jan, chatting with Grandma, getting the tea ready, even cooking an evening meal for those who were able to eat!

TRUE FRIENDSHIP

Tenacious, practical, loyal support is one of the most valuable gifts that one Christian can give another. As we assess our gifts and move out into new areas of ministry we need the honest and loving support of friends. We need to know that there are people we can always count on. True friendship shows itself in practical ways, in faithful prayer support and in public backing.

Paul was certainly not so spiritual that he didn't feel the cold or become dejected and suffer loneliness when no friends were around. His letters show a real mixture of the deeply spiritual and the very practical:

> 'Do your best to come to me quickly, for Demas, because he loved this world, has deserted me. . . Only Luke is with me. Get Mark and bring him with you, because he is helpful to me in my ministry. . . When you come, bring the cloak that I left with Carpus at Troas, and my scrolls, especially the parchments.
>
> Alexander the metalworker did me a great deal of harm. . . You too should be on your guard against him, because he strongly opposed our message.
>
> At my first defence, no one came to my support, but everyone deserted me. May it not be held against them. But the Lord stood at my side and gave me strength, so that through me the message might be fully proclaimed and all the Gentiles might hear it. . .
>
> Greet Priscilla and Aquila and the household of Onesiphorus. . . Do your best to get here before winter. . .' *2 Timothy 4:9–21*

Phygellus and Hermogenes had deserted Paul when he most needed them. Onesiphorus was a complete contrast. His name meant 'profit-bearing' and he was obviously profitable to Paul! He was not ashamed of Paul when he was in prison; on the contrary, he was prepared to risk his own reputation by visiting and helping him.

Practical friendship

True friendship is very practical. 'It's pretty cold here!' says Paul. 'So come before winter and bring my winter cloak; don't miss the boat or I'll freeze! I need your support, brother! Others have deserted me so it's bad enough spiritually, but it's worse feeling cold!'

When we say, 'Yes, I'll pray for you,' we need to be prepared to add, 'And what can I give you to help?' Good ministry always remembers the whole person. People are not just 'souls with ears' but have physical, emotional and social needs as well. We must not be so heavenly minded that we are of no earthly use to each other!

We hear an echo of the experience and words of Jesus as Paul goes on to say, 'At my first defence, no-one came to my support, but everyone deserted me. May it not be held against them.' Friendship keeps its side of the relationship open, even if the other person has broken off communication. In similar, though more extreme circumstances, Jesus had said, 'Father, forgive them, for they do not know what they are doing' (Luke 23:34).

Loyal friendship

Secondly, like the love Paul describes in 1 Corinthians 13, friendship is about loyal support. It's easy to give our support to one another as long as the other person is doing exactly what we want! It's easy to support our housegroup leader as long as she is leading the group the way we want it led! But as soon as she takes it in a slightly different direction or does something we are not too happy with, our loyalty backs off.

Time and again I have seen churches where this has happened. Influential groups in the church have given loyalty to a pastor, deacon or leader as long as he toes their particular line but woe betide him if what he thinks God is saying doesn't happen to further their own interests! Suddenly they are not the strong friends they seemed to be. Their support is withdrawn.

Paul's call to Timothy and to us is to show a radically different sort of friendship. Paul knew that the pressures facing Timothy were intense; he knew that supporting a man in prison would not make him popular among those Christians in Ephesus who were concerned about what their neighbours might think.

God's call comes to us today through these words of Paul. 'Never mind what other people will think! You – John, Anita, Puddlemarsh-in-the-Hole Church – you be faithful, loyal and committed to your brothers and sisters in Christ, in the good times and in the bad. Make sure that you are like Onesiphorus, that your friendship is real and rich.'

WHAT FRIENDS ARE FOR

In the friendships recorded in the Bible we can see a number of ways in which a friend proved crucial to someone's ministry.

To restore perspective

A good friend can help to restore our focus on God when the pressures of life have distorted our perspective. Recent surveys have shown that church ministers suffer from one of the highest levels of stress. Depression and a dogged sense of failure are common visitors.

David, on the run from Saul, knew what this was like. If ever a man was under stress for a prolonged period of time it was him! Knowing that God's plan was for him to become king – David had been anointed king some years earlier – he must have experienced intense frustration while he waited for it to happen. During this anxious, foggy time in David's life, we read that, 'Saul's son Jonathan went to David . . . and helped him to find strength in God.' (1 Samuel 23:16).

When we feel pressured from all sides and don't know which way to turn, it is good to have a friend who will say, 'Slow down; just wait for the Lord to act.

He knows what he wants to do with your gifts and he'll see that it gets done in good time.'

To provide practical help

As widows, Ruth and Naomi needed each other. Naomi had the wisdom to know how to survive but Ruth, being younger, had the energy to do the hard work of gleaning in the fields.[6]

Paul commented of John Mark that 'he is helpful to me in my ministry'.[7] Paul had found that the two of them, working together, could accomplish more than either could single-handed. It is good to have a friend who is more experienced than yourself who can help you work out problems that crop up in the course of your ministry.

To give encouragement

Friends can encourage us as we work out our ministries, perhaps pledging support for a bold move or encouraging us to keep going when things get difficult. In the Old Testament Joshua and Caleb encouraged Moses to fulfil his vision for entering the promised land.[8]

Later, living under a king who banned faith in God, Shadrach, Meshach and Abednego stood together in solidarity when threatened with death for their faith.[9]

When Daniel offered to use his gift of discernment to tell King Nebuchadnezzar what his dream meant, it was to his three friends that he turned for prayer, support and encouragement.[10]

And when Paul was afraid and despondent, Jesus himself drew near to encourage him: 'the Lord stood at my side and gave me strength'.[11]

To challenge each other

At one time, Paul felt he had to challenge John Mark's commitment to the missionary work he had been called to do. That was a tough time for Mark but the challenge bore fruit. Paul's whole letter is, in effect, a challenge to Timothy, setting out the standards of ministry and of personal life that God requires.

As Christians today we are under big pressures. We see those whose Christian commitment we once admired now far from God and it makes us wonder if it is worth our while continuing. When people in our church fellowships say or do things that are less than the best, we easily follow their example. The lowest common denominator is always the most comfortable one to live with. It is all the more important, then, to have friends who will sharpen us up, keep us faithful to our calling and have the temerity to see that we are staying spiritually healthy!

Writing in *Christianity Today* after the fall of a top Christian leader, David Augsburger comments on the need for all Christians to have close friends to whom they are accountable:

'Accountability, puzzling as the concept is in the modern situation, is the mark of maturity in discipleship. It is not optional, nor a mere by-product. It is essential, central and definitive of life in the community of the Spirit'.[12]

When someone fails and his Christian life begins to fall apart we find it much easier to back off from him and withhold the loyalty and love which we once gave him when he walked with God. It is as if we feel he is dirty or unclean and we don't want to be contaminated by contact with him. But why should our friendship and loyalty be conditional on people behaving in a certain way? Are we more concerned about their well-being or about our 'purity'?

It is important that we do not 'dump' our friends when they fail or do something of which we do not approve. If our message of forgiveness through Jesus is to mean anything we need to love those who fail, caring for them and bringing them back to full fellowship with Christ. In the body of Christ there must be a passionate commitment to one another that goes beyond the ordinary into the extraordinary.

How can we develop the sort of friendships that will be helpful in our ministries and in our Christian walk in general? There are three areas that we need to think about:

- *Ongoing friendship*. We need to give ourselves time

to relax! One of the best ways of relaxing is to spend time in the company of friends who like the same sort of recreation – going to the cinema, eating, arguing about current issues, playing squash, or whatever. It is important that we stay the sort of people with whom others can relax and let their hair down, and that we are able to drop 'professionalism' and formality when we are with them. It is also important to maintain friendships with people outside the church fellowship; it is surprisingly easy to let such friendships get choked out by church activities and 'Christian busyness'.

It is crucial to know that your friends are your friends because you are you, not because of what you do or for what you can give them. Without this sort of confidence in others, friendship can turn into simply another sort of test that adds to stress and tension. The best way to ensure that your friends do think of you this way is, of course, to be that sort of friend to them!

● *Crisis friendship*. Over the course of our lives it is only with a handful of people that we develop really strong friendships that stand the tests of time and distance. These are precious friends to have. They are the sort who will not give up on you even if everyone else does. If they were to discover that you were tragically, cultivating an extra-marital relationship or embezzling church funds, these friends would certainly challenge you – but they would also continue to love you. It is important to make ourselves accountable to such people, perhaps organising get-togethers with them every couple of months or so and giving each other the freedom to ask probing questions about our lives and the way we are using our gifts.

● *Support group friendship*. Support groups are small groups of people who share a common task or goal and who meet regularly for mutual prayer support, encouragement and sharing. It is particularly important to belong to such a group if you are in any 'front-line' Christian ministry – any sort of evangelistic, teaching or pastoral work. Ministers' 'fraternals' rarely, in my experience, do the work of a support group. Their concern is usually more with business matters, especially the business of running the fraternal! If you find yourself in this situation, don't be afraid to admit your need of a greater depth of sharing and support and begin to sound out others who may be interested in forming such a group with you.

7

GROWING
THE GIFT OF
PREACHING

Atheistic governments can't stifle it, philosophers can't ignore it, theologians can't argue it away. *Nothing* can rob the gospel of its truth or of its power to change lives and point people to the living God.

Because the gospel will never be out of date or made obsolete by something better, it is exciting to be called like Timothy to the ministry of proclaiming it to others. But it can also be daunting! What does this particular ministry involve and how can we grow our gifts for it?

As an apostle, Paul had the unique task of explaining to the first Christians exactly what it was Jesus had done. He taught them in such a way that they could pass on the message of the gospel to all subsequent generations: '. . . of this gospel I was appointed a herald and an apostle and a teacher' (2 Timothy 1:11). Since Paul's day, God has called other people with gifts for communication to continue the task of passing it on and of making sure that people understand what they hear. This was the commission that Paul gave to Timothy:

> 'What you have heard from me, keep as the pattern of sound teaching, with faith and love in Christ Jesus. Guard the good deposit that was entrusted to you – guard it with the help of the Holy Spirit who lives in us.'
>
> *2 Timothy 1:13–14*

Paul had invested his teaching and a great deal of his life in Timothy. In this way he had deposited the gospel into his care.

PREACH TRUTH

It is very tempting to preach about almost anything so long as it interests people. In this last decade of the twentieth century, materialism and self-fulfilment have become two key concerns; any preaching which offers wealth, personal fulfilment and happiness as part of the Christian package is likely to attract followers in large numbers. There is a growing interest in a gospel which basically says, 'God exists to make me happy.' But God's specific command to Timothy was to 'preach the word'. This may not always be the same as preaching what people want to hear:

> 'In the presence of God and of Christ Jesus, who will judge the living and the dead, and in

view of his appearing and his kingdom, I give you this charge: Preach the Word; be prepared in season and out of season; correct, rebuke and encourage – with great patience and careful instruction. For the time will come when men will not put up with sound doctrine. Instead, to suit their own desires, they will gather around them a great number of teachers to say what their itching ears want to hear. They will turn their ears away from the truth and turn aside to myths. But you, keep your head in all situations, endure hardship, do the work of an evangelist, discharge all the duties of your ministry.'   *2 Timothy 4:1–5*

Paul's charge to Timothy could not have been more serious. It is something like a court scene. When someone is called to give evidence in court, she has to place one hand on the Bible or the Scripture of her religion and say, 'I swear by Almighty God that the evidence I give shall be the truth, the whole truth and nothing but the truth.' It is as if Paul here has one hand on the Old Testament Scriptures to indicate that God is witness to the truth of what he is going on to write. Paul charges Timothy with a heavy responsibility: to make sure that people know what God has done in Christ, to bring them into his kingdom and to teach them how to live in a way that honours God.

The task is urgent: when Christ comes back it will be in judgement – both on how faithfully we have carried out this ministry and on the response of those who have heard. I can imagine Timothy thinking, in his less spiritual moments, 'Oh, Jesus isn't going to come back *now*, not just yet, not while I'm a young pastor! Maybe at the end of my ministry he will; but here? Now? Surely not!'

Once when Jan and I were in the States we flew from Lubbock, Texas, to Wichita, Kansas – about six-hundred miles. I'd never been to Wichita before and knew only two people there out of its five hundred thousand inhabitants. We taxied in and the couple met us at the airport. Before long, Janet was resting in our hosts' home and I was in the local Christian book shop! While we were there, my host was called away on his pager and I was left alone to wander around the shop thinking how great it was to be six thousand miles away from home, knowing no one!

Just then, someone tapped me on the shoulder and said, 'Steve Gaukroger, isn't it?' 'Pardon?' was the only thing I could think of saying as I turned to see who it was. The stranger standing there told me that, about a year earlier and six hundred miles away, he had been present at the wedding of Janet's sister, which I had conducted. I was absolutely amazed! All Jan could say when I told her, was, 'Good job you were behaving yourself, then, wasn't it?!'

There was no way I could have met someone there who knew me – but I did! Sometimes we need to be jolted out of our complacency by the reminder that

Jesus could arrive at any moment and challenge all that we are doing. The living God *will* one day speak to us face to face. In view of that, we need to soak our lives in the word of God and preach it powerfully and effectively. We must tell people exactly what it teaches and dare not let them have any doubts about its requirements or its promises. At the same time, our work, homes and worship need to be alive and rich with God's presence *now*.

PREACH TO CHANGE LIVES

The aim of preaching is to help people bring their lives more fully under God's control, whether those people are already committed to Christ, are in the church but not really living out their faith, have distanced themselves from the church or have not yet been reached for Christ. Paul gives Timothy a number of principles to live by in his work as a preacher, teacher and pastor.

Correct, rebuke and encourage

'*Correcting*' means to channel people's thinking; it is about teaching. Timothy was to be a road sign to right thinking, showing drivers which streets were one-way, how to get from the by-pass onto the motorway or which way to go round the roundabout. Paul warned him that members of his congregation would wander off into all kinds of heresies. Timothy was to correct them, guiding them back onto the path, putting up road signs which said, 'No entry', 'Turn right here', 'Go round this way'.

'Show them the way to go,' is Paul's commission. Without this kind of ministry today, many vulnerable Christians, particularly young people, will end up as Moonies, Mormons or Jehovah's Witnesses. The fringes of Christianity are fertile fields for the cults. People are attracted to them because of their strong personal relationships, their overwhelming expressions of love and care, and their one-on-one discipleship. We need to be giving very clear, specific teaching so that people can discern truth from error. And this teaching needs to be backed up by the warmth of our fellowship. This needs to be deep and genuine if the loneliness and isolation felt by many today are to be met with the love of Christ.

'*Rebuke*' is another thing that Paul charges Timothy to do. This has to do with behaviour, rather than teaching: 'Timothy, there will be people whose behaviour doesn't tie up with God's word and what it says. Don't be frightened to rebuke them; not, of course, in a spirit of anger or as if you were dealing with a little child. Simply be clear about what kind of behaviour is wrong.' Perhaps someone has a tendency to gossip or is refusing to speak to another member of the church family, or is skilfully deceiving the tax man! People need to know where God and his church stand on these issues. We must lovingly and gently tell them.

'*Encourage.*' The preaching ministry has some-times got itself a bad name because of a heavy-handed, guilt-inducing emphasis on 'oughts': 'Be nice to your wife. Be a good neighbour. Get out there witnessing! Be kind, be loving, pray more, study the Bible harder!' The vast majority of people in our congregations will already have a keen sense of their own failures and further reminder of them will simply drive them further from the saving grace of Christ. In her book, *Searching for lost coins*[13], Ann Loades quotes a poem called *You are not enough*, written by an American college student. She introduces it like this:

'After father, mother, husband and children have all told her why whatever she does for them is not enough, we have:

"It is not enough
said her pastor
that you
    teach the second graders
    change the cloths and candles
    kneel prostrate at the altar
as long as there are starving children in the world
you must
not eat
without guilt." '

Receiving encouragement is an essential part of Christian growth. It is important to assure people that God has already fully accepted them. In his sight we are already images of Christ, possessing every quality necessary to be God's children.

Church leaders are by no means immune from this feeling of being inadequate, of not doing enough. I have led a number of leadership training seminars over the last few years and am convinced that much of what people need is not 'know how' but simple encouragement. I am amazed at the number of church leaders who will come to me at the end of these training weeks and say, 'If it hadn't been for this week I was thinking of resigning from my church commitments.'

People at the very brink of leaving the ministry can be encouraged and re-enthused by something as simple as a note I once received from a deacon in the church. All it said was, 'I just wanted to say that I really appreciate all your love and support.' Encouragement can make all the difference.

Teach with patience and care

A church that affects its community is one that is built up over many years 'with great patience and careful instruction.' As individuals draw on the Holy Spirit's power and are renewed in him, and as they come to emotional and mental maturity, the church is strengthened.

Careful instruction and great patience are necessary because there will come a time, says Paul, when people won't come to hear preaching from the Bible but will go from event to event and from teacher to teacher looking for the latest formula for instant success in the Christian life.

I meet them at events like Spring Harvest. I call them 'Spring Harvest Groupies'. They go to celebration events up and down the country – Spring Harvest is only one of them. But when you sit down and ask them what is happening in the place where they live and worship, you sometimes find that they're not even going to church! They're thrilled by the worship and the atmosphere of a great 'celebration' event but are not making their faith count where it hurts in the experience of their day-to-day life.

It is marvellously exhilarating to be at the big conferences but the main point of going is to learn from those we hear there and to bring the heart of what they say back into the ground-work of our church fellowships. If their teaching doesn't work in your local community, it doesn't work! Something can sound very powerful in the emotionally-charged atmosphere of a big meeting but it might be pretty useless in the nitty-gritty of daily work and life.

I have also been saddened to see people following all the different fads and fashions of Christian leadership. In the early 1970s when 'renewal' came on the scene, people went to hear Christian leaders speak about the Holy Spirit. When that became a bit passé they wandered on to 'healing'. 'Signs and wonders' was the next thing but now it is not quite so high on the agenda. As that fades people are on the look-out for the next rising star, as if we can just drop one thing and pick up another, never letting any of them really change our souls. Our task, as was Timothy's, is to draw such people back into a whole-hearted commitment to the body of Christ.

In any community you will find another group of people – 'born again' Christians who are no longer worshipping with a church fellowship and who do not intend to. If you ask why, you will discover that something happened in their lives in the past and they feel the church acted in response to it in a hurtful or inappropriate way. Sometimes the cause of hurt is really quite trivial, or there may have been no way the pastor or other members of the church could have known about it anyway:

Pastor and Doctor

Mrs Huff is up the miff tree,
 On a seat fixed good and firm;
And she'd like to tell the pastor
 A few things to make him squirm.

Mrs Huff was sick abed, sir,
    Yes, sir, sick abed a week!
And the pastor didn't call, sir,
    Never even took a peek.

When I asked her if the doctor
    Called to see her she said, 'Sure.'
And she looked as if she thought I
    Needed some good mental cure.

Then I asked her how the doctor
    Knew that sickness laid her low.
And she said that she had called him
    On the phone and told him so.

Now the doctor gets his bill paid
    With a nicely written check;
But the pastor, for not knowing,
    Simply gets it in the neck.

                    (*Author unknown*)

Often, of course, the fault does lie with the church: someone made an insensitive remark or failed to follow up what was obviously a cry for help. But some people haven't worshipped with other Christians for three, five, even twenty years because of some dispute over a building project or because they can't find a church that exactly fits their needs. They are denying the body the chance to be helped and encouraged by their gifts and abilities and are denying themselves the chance to grow in God by being a part of his people. It is our task to go out and find them, to call them back and to seek to heal the wounds.

Be consistent

If we are to teach God's truth and if those who hear it are to live it, there needs to be consistency on both sides.

The word of God has to be preached and lived 'in season and out of season.' Other translations render this as 'whether the time is right or not' (Good News Bible) and whether 'convenient or inconvenient' (New English Bible). As a pastor I have to preach God's word when I feel like it and when I don't; when I am supported and praised and when I am criticised.

If you are one of those people who are significantly affected by your moods, you will know how difficult this impartial consistency is! If you are feeling discouraged, getting over the 'flu or have problems at home, preparing a sermon can be a real struggle. The last thing you want to do is face the church at all, let alone lead them in worship. At times like these, we need to remember that Jesus is Lord, not our feelings. The test of a pastor's ministry is not whether he or she can preach the word occasionally but whether, day by day and week by week, he or she can minister faithfully, whatever the pressure.

The principle applies to all Christians. We need to be consistent and faithful in our Christian living – in our home life, at work and in the tasks we take on at church. Some people have a history of doing one job after another for the life of the church, full of enthusiasm to start with but sticking at it only for a month or two. Consistency is the key to Christian ministry and one of the marks of Christian maturity – going on ministering through the good times and the bad ones. There is no 'closed season' on it!

There is a geyser in Yellowstone Park in America called 'Old Faithful'. It erupts every sixty-one minutes. That's pretty consistent for an old geyser! Others are far more spectacular, erupting once a month – if you are lucky. But, of course, you have to stand there for a month to be sure of seeing them! 'Old Faithful' is not that spectacular but you know that if you arrive at the site you will not have to wait more than sixty-one minutes to see it.

Be committed to growth

'Do the work of an evangelist' is Paul's next command. But in explaining this, notice that he doesn't say to Timothy, 'Try to find out whether you're gifted as an evangelist.' He says, 'Make sure your people know that it is right to tell others about Jesus – *and make it happen*!' In other words, 'Find the evangelistic gifts in the fellowship', not 'Be out every evening knocking at people's doors and giving them tracts.'

As pastors we can become so concerned about maintenance that we forget the concept of mission. How many people in your church fellowship are involved with 'looking after the saints' and how many are reaching out to those who do not yet know Jesus? If we added up our figures, we would probably find that there are thousands of people engaged in maintaining the Body – in pastoral care, singing in the choir, making coffee – and hardly any in the task of evangelism. Let's reverse that trend and commit ourselves to seeing God's church grow.

It was William Temple who said, 'The church is the only institution that exists for the benefit of its non-members.' The trouble is that we are under a lot of pressure today to be linked only with people who are like us – people who dress the same way, who live in the same sort of houses, who speak the same way, who spend their money on the same sort of things and send their children to the same sort of school. And this pressure carries over into church life. Even if those from outside our social grouping join the church, the temptation is always to make them become like us, rather than like Christ.

The commission Jesus left his followers was to win the world for him. A church that is not growing numerically is probably not being faithful to that commission. It is sometimes said in defence of static churches that we are not called to be successful but to be faithful. But, if we are being faithful we will, in general, be successful in terms of numerical growth, so it is right to aim for this. It is also crucial to set specific goals for growth. As it has been pointed out on many a car sticker: 'Aim at nothing and you are sure to hit it!'

There are situations, of course, where sociological factors make growth very hard but these are relatively rare. William Carey for instance, a Baptist missionary who went to India in 1793, was there seven years before baptising his first convert. But the problems that hampered the work of Carey and those other first missionaries to India were ones linked with culture shock and the physical rigours of adapting to a totally different climate and way of life. Today, we can draw on many studies of church growth and on insights into presenting the gospel across barriers of culture and language to help us bring people into the kingdom. And it is worth noting that, despite all the setbacks and difficulties he faced, William Carey's watchword was always, 'Attempt great things for God. Expect great things from God.'

PREACH TO YOURSELF

Paul's letter to Timothy is shot through with reminders that everything he tells other people must first be tested on himself, like a doctor taking his own medicine or a cook sitting down to eat with the staff in the canteen. If Timothy expected his church members to live the truth, he himself had to handle the Bible with integrity. If they were to become Christlike in character he, too, was to 'avoid godless chatter' and quarrelling. If he expected them to demonstrate holiness he, too, was to 'flee the evil desires of youth.' When we point at others we should take note that three fingers are pointing back at us!

I often find myself convicted by my own preaching! Presenting others with God's requirements, all the while knowing how far short I myself fall of reaching them, brings a tremendous sense of guilt with it. But, in our personal living and in our thinking we need constantly to be on our guard. As Paul warned Timothy in his first letter to him, 'Watch your life and doctrine closely.' What we teach and how we live go hand-in-hand and each has an effect on the other. It may be that Paul had Demas in mind when he wrote that warning to Timothy. His story is one that should make us stop and think about how firm our commitment is both to right living and right doctrine.

The Demas experience

Demas is mentioned only three times in the Bible, but those three mentions give us a potted life history of a leading member of Paul's 'ministry team' that is devastating.

In Philemon 24 Paul refers to Demas as one of his team of 'fellow-workers', along with Mark, Aristarchus and Luke. He is obviously working hard alongside Paul, who is imprisoned in Ephesus, to bring the kingdom of God to the people of that city and to strengthen the newly-established church there.

At the end of his letter to the Christians in Colossae Paul mentions him again – but it is only a passing reference. He speaks about Tychicus, 'a dear brother, a faithful minister and a fellow-servant in the Lord'; about Aristarchus, Mark and Justus who 'have proved a comfort to me'; about Epaphras, who 'is always wrestling in prayer for you'; our 'dear friend' Luke – 'and Demas.' Demas is still around, but there is a hint that his spiritual passion is cooling.

Then, in 2 Timothy 4:10 we read, 'Demas, because he loved this world, has deserted me.'

These three references give us a picture of a person sliding away from God. In any church, and among any group of ministers, there may be people at all three stages of the 'Demas experience'. Some are giving all they are to God, wanting to love him, be faithful to him and to work with him. Others have known what it is like to feel that way but now feel something of an empty shell. There may be others who are still there, doing the job for the sake of appearances, but have actually stopped walking with God.

There is a wealth of sadness in Paul's comment on Demas. He feels it keenly as a great desertion. His words echo something of the sadness that Jesus felt at the desertions of Judas and Peter – the two people who, in their different ways, probably hurt Jesus more than anyone else. Peter had not only been part of the twelve but part of the three, the intimate circle with whom Jesus had shared his heart.

Peter, Judas and Demas give us hard-hitting reminders that even those in the so-called 'inner circle of faith' are not immune to the appeal of the world and the temptations of Satan to draw us away from the heart of God. In 1 Corinthians 10:12 Paul put it like this, 'So, if you think you are standing firm, be careful that you don't fall!'

Often, being in pastoral ministry keeps us well aware of the possibility of falling into the same trap as Demas, as we have the task of trying to prevent it happening in others. In fact, our problem can be more that of thinking we're not likely to fare any better! But Paul opened his letter by encouraging Timothy to be faithful and he concludes it by showing that it is possible to be so, as we shall see in the next chapter.

8
HELD
BY
GOD

'I have fought the good fight, I have finished
the race, I have kept the faith. Now there is in
store for me the crown of righteousness, which
the Lord, the righteous Judge, will award to
me on that day – and not only to me, but also
to all who have longed for his appearing.'
2 Timothy 4:7–8

Taking a picture from the Olympic Games Paul says, 'I
prepared. I trained. I ran. What's more, I've now finished the race and God is going to give me the gold
medal for my performance. I have kept the faith and
am going to hear God's, "Well done!"'

Paul's claim sounds almost arrogant to us. How
can we find the confidence to keep growing and using
our gifts with the sort of certainty and joyful hope that
Paul seemed to have? We need to look more closely at
the grounds for his confidence.

A LOVING HEAVENLY FATHER

When our oldest daughter was about two years old we had a little 'game'. I would say to her, 'Stand on your head, Bethany!' And she would get down and put her head on the floor. Then I'd say, 'Now lift your hands up.' So she would be there, with her head and feet on the floor and her arms out wide. Brilliant! Wonderful stuff! And then I'd ask, 'Are you all right?' and try to slip out of the room while she wasn't looking. But the second I stopped paying attention or wandered off, she would yell, 'Daddy, look! Daddy, look!' So I'd make a big show of her because she was trying to please me. She didn't really *want* to stand on her head!

Most of us, if we are honest, let our lives be dominated by trying to please people. Perhaps it is our wife or husband we want to please – if only because it leads to a quiet life! It may be the boss at work, the neighbours who don't like our garden looking so scruffy or people at church who expect us to be more Christlike than we really are. We can feel driven by their expectations and believe that the only way to a peaceful life is to comply with their spoken or unspoken demands. In addition, most of us want to be well thought of, respected and looked up to and some of us will do the equivalent of standing on our heads to make sure that we are!

But the good news of the gospel is that we *don't*

need to. Ultimately, the only person whom it is important to please is God. And he is our loving heavenly Father who accepts us already just as we are. We need never lose confidence that he loves us, no matter what we do. When we let the reality of this sink into us it will take away all the self-doubts, the anxiety that we cannot do the job to which God has called us, and the feelings of worthlessness. As our Father and Creator who continues to work in us, God never doubts our abilities, potential and value.

A GOD WHO UPHOLDS

There are times when we feel very much aware of our inability to keep up our Christian ministry and witness in our own strength. Paul may have been able to win the fight, run the race and keep the faith but are we made of the same stuff as Paul? Paul was someone special, anyway – or so we think. We can understand that God would persevere with him but is he really going to do the same for me?

Time and again we realise we have botched things up; our eyes were not on serving God but on some other goal. But in the middle of all our failures and struggles, temptations and pressures, God invites us to come to him and say, 'Lord, I've fallen again but I really do want to be faithful and consistent in my walk with you.' And he will pick us up and set us on the track again.

Think about it. He is a God of second, third and ninety-fifth chances. He is *even more determined than you are* that you should serve him faithfully and well in the ministry he's given you, and that you should find your greatest fulfilment in doing so. If you ever have doubts about that, think over what he has already done for you and, with Paul, ask yourself,

> 'If God is for us, who can be against us? He who did not spare his own Son, but gave him up for us all – how will he not also, along with him, graciously give us all things?'
>
> *Romans 8:31–32*

As we step out in faith, *he* will provide all the faith and perseverance we need to carry out all that he asks us to do. And, when we have done so, we will hear the great 'Well done!' from the King of the universe. That's an exciting prospect!

> '. . . the Lord stood at my side and gave me strength, so that through me the message might be fully proclaimed and all the Gentiles might hear it. And I was delivered from the lion's mouth. The Lord will rescue me from every evil attack and will bring me safely to his heavenly kingdom. To him be glory for ever and ever. Amen.'
>
> *2 Timothy 4:17–18*

IDENTIFYING YOUR GIFTS

Read the following points and give yourself a mark out of 5 for each. If you give yourself 5 it will be one of your very strong points. If you give yourself 0 or 1 it will be one of your very weak points.

Then transfer the marks that you give yourself to the appropriate squares in the chart. The number in each square corresponds to the point number in the list below.

___ 1 I am very good at listening.

___ 2 I enjoy explaining things to others from the Bible.

___ 3 I love preaching or talking about Jesus to a congregation or group.

___ 4 I am often used to bring others to Christ.

___ 5 I enjoy administrative work.

___ 6 I feel a deep, caring love for those who are ill, and feel a call to help them get well.

— 7 I am handy at most things and adaptable.

— 8 I am deeply concerned about the world and social affairs.

— 9 I am usually looked to for a lead.

— 10 I make helpful relationships with others easily.

— 11 Others are helped when I teach them things.

— 12 I love the study and work in preparing a message.

— 13 God has given me a great love for others and a longing to win them for him.

— 14 I can organise well, clearly and efficiently.

— 15 Others find my presence soothing and healing.

— 16 I like helping other people.

— 17 I am active in service in the community.

— 18 In a group I am often elected chairperson or leader.

— 19 I can encourage others and help bear burdens.

— 20 I love study and finding the facts.

— 21 People tell me that they find my sermons a blessing.

— 22 I find my life is full of opportunities to witness to Christ.

___ 23 I love doing office work and do it thoroughly.

___ 24 I have sometimes laid hands on the sick and they have been helped.

___ 25 I am a practical type.

___ 26 I am very aware of the needs of society today and feel called to do something about them.

___ 27 When leading something I put a lot of preparation into it.

___ 28 I really care about other people.

___ 29 I have patience in helping others understand Christian things.

___ 30 I feel a clear call to preach.

___ 31 I love to talk to others about Jesus.

___ 32 I am painstaking about details in organisation.

___ 33 I spend time praying with and for sick people.

___ 34 I spend much time helping others in practical ways.

___ 35 I feel God is at work in the world today and I must work along with him there.

___ 36 I am good at delegating work to others in a team setting.

1	10	19	28	**A**
2	11	20	29	**B**
3	12	21	30	**C**
4	13	22	31	**D**
5	14	23	32	**E**
6	15	24	33	**F**
7	16	25	34	**G**
8	17	26	35	**H**
9	18	27	36	**I**

Add up the totals along each line and place them in the lettered box at the end of the column.

If your highest total is in column:

A your gift is pastoral

B   "   "   " teaching

C   "   "   " preaching

D   "   "   " evangelism

E   "   "   " administration

F   "   "   " healing

G   "   "   " giving practical help

H   "   "   " service to society

I   "   "   " leadership

A and **F** (pastoral and healing gifts) are primarily the 'caring' gifts.

B, **C** and **D** (teaching, preaching and evangelism) are primarily the 'thinking and talking' gifts.

E, **G**, **H** and **I** (administration, giving practical help, service to society and leadership) are primarily the 'doing' gifts.

It is easy to mislead yourself in this sort of exercise; we are not always fully aware of our own strengths. So, besides filling it in yourself, it may be helpful to give a copy of the questionnaire to four of your closest friends and ask them to fill it in for you (ie, changing each of the statements to 'he/she', 'he is/she is' etc) as honestly as possible. Don't show them your marks until after you have theirs.

(This gift-identification questionnaire was devised by Lewis Misselbrook.)

NOTES

Chapter 3

1 David Watson, *Discipleship*. London: Hodder and Stoughton, 1989.

2 John Stott, *The Message of 2 Timothy: Guard the Gospel*. Leicester: IVP, 1984.

Chapter 4

3 Commentaries, Bible Dictionaries and Concordances are the basic books you will need for this library. You will also find it helpful to build up a collection of books that explain:
- how to interpret the different types of literature in the Bible (eg *Unlock the Bible*, by Stephen Motyer)
- how to tackle Bible study (eg *Get more from your Bible*, by Brian Abshire)
- how to lead and facilitate small groups (eg *Good things come in small groups*, by various authors; *Growing Christians in small groups*, by John Mallison; *Leading Bible discussions*, by J Nyquist and J Kuhatschek – *Lifebuilder* series).

All of these are published by Scripture Union.

4 William Barclay, *Timothy, Titus and Philemon* from the Daily Study Bible. Edinburgh: The Saint Andrew Press.

Chapter 5

5 Christians differ over their views of what will happen at the end times. The concept of an idyllic period of one thousand years derives from Revelation 20:6. Pre-millennialists are those who believe Christ will return before this thousand-year period. Post-millennialists believe he will return after it. A-millennialists believe that the reference to one thousand years should be taken symbolically, not literally.

Chapter 6

6 See Ruth 2:2.

7 2 Timothy 4:11.

8 Numbers 13:30.

9 Daniel 3.

10 Daniel 2:17–19.

11 2 Timothy 4:17.

12 David Augsburger, *Christianity Today*, 20 November 1987.

Chapter 7

13 Ann Loades, *Searching for Lost Coins*. London: SPCK, 1987.